The Roots of the Self

Also by Robert Ornstein

The Roots of the Self

Unraveling the Mystery of Who We Are

Robert Ornstein

Illustrations by Ted Dewan

HarperSanFrancisco

A Division of HarperCollinsPublishers

FIRST EDITION

Illustrations by Ted Dewan

Library of Congress Cataloging-in-Publication Data
Ornstein, Robert E. (Robert Evan)
    The roots of the self: unraveling the mystery of who we are /
    Robert Ornstein. — 1st ed.
        p. cm.
    Includes bibliographical references and index.
    ISBN 0–06–250788–5 (alk. paper) — ISBN 0–06–250789–3 (pbk.)
    1. Self.   2. Personality.   3. Individual differences.   4. Neuropsychology.
    I. title.
    BF697.065 1993
    155.2—dc20   92–56116
                                                                      CIP

93   94   95   96   97   ❖ HAD   10   9   8   7   6   5   4   3   2   1

This edition is printed on acid-free paper that meets the American National Standards Institute Z39.48 Standard.

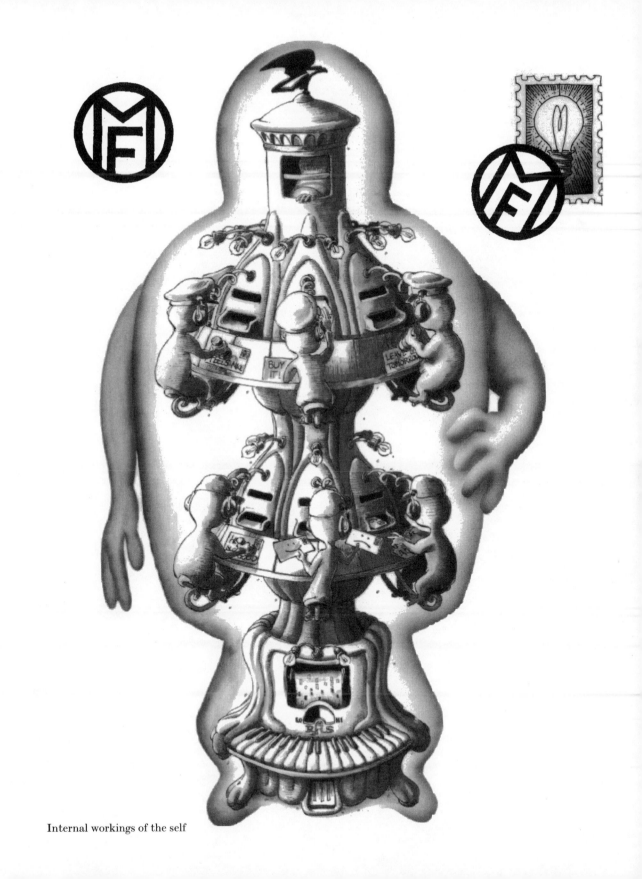

Internal workings of the self

Contents

The Roots of the Self

Chapter 1

Introduction

The Puzzle of Individuality

It must have been 1947 or 1948.

I was trying to sleep, but my parents had company. My father's friend was explaining some of the theories about the person that were au courant in postwar New York:

"There's Sid" (I'm still sure that this is what he said), "there's the eagle, and there is the super-eagle, and each of them fights for control."

I knew a Sid who was a friend of my father's, but *this* "Sid" was more like Steve Martin's "wild and crazy kind of guy." The eagle, on the other hand, went forth bravely to organize one's life, while the super-eagle, the super-eagle. Well, I never grasped that one since I got too excited about it. I knew immediately that this was the one I wanted to be. I could see myself soaring over everything. And in my mind, over and over, I could hear the cry:

"Here comes the super-eagle!"

*A*nd then there was the inevitable time when I found out I was misinformed about this, and when I also found out the truth about Santa Claus.

1

Even before this discovery my young mind had made a good case for the usefulness of dividing the person into these three particular parts. Sid, I assumed, tried frantic things, the eagle advanced in life, and when things went wrong there was the amazing super-eagle who would swoop in and save the day.

In retrospect, this concept wasn't so much worse in accounting for the phenomena of the person than many of the more standard divisions of personality. After all, many of the most influential interpretations of the self stem from just such personal conceptions. The thinkers who have become household names may or may not have had professional training, they may or may not have been well informed, and their theories may or may not be functional.

In our own minds, we, too, tend to arrange people into groups, using such categories as excitable, placid, hot, cool, impulsive, disorderly, or controlled. Formal systems use different categories to try to explain individuality, whether those categories include the super-ego, the "wise old man" or "what's your sign." There must be millions of personality-typing systems, based on everything from skin color to eye color to universal archetypes; the time, day, or date of birth; body type or even blood type; and whether we are choleric, melancholic, Aquarius, introverted, extroverted, or something else.

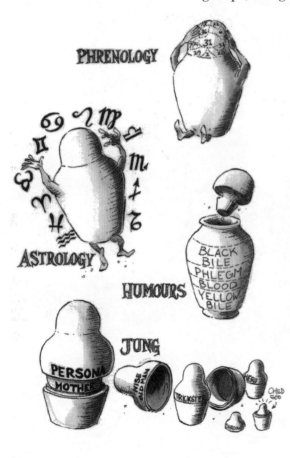

Ideas for personality classifications, such as id, ego, and superego, may originate from the observations of brilliant scientists. They may come from clinical or biological or casual observation. The theories gain a hold and become part of the language until one knows what to expect from a Leo, an antisocial personality, a redhead, a mesomorph, or one fixated at the oral stage of development. And these observations and classifications are often interesting and functional. They provide everyone from small children to clinical psychiatrists with a routine for classifying people, one that helps us make sense of ourselves and others.

But that's all they do, since one system doesn't map on to the other, and thus people of different cultures, cults, eras, areas, sciences, and nonsciences have made feeble progress in developing an understanding of the self. The concept of the person can be seen to occupy a "three-dimensional space" (in the mathematical sense), and this space can be filled with almost any three independent assumptions—the vaguer, the better. Personal trouble may mean that the person is possessed by evil spirits, or that a multiple personality is acting up, or the moon is out of joint. We need an explanation to get through the day, and that is what most personality-typing systems provide.

One's own self can't be known in the way one knows one's hair color or height, or even **IQ**. Human beings do not have, I believe, a "true self" that they can discover by searching through their minds or their experiences. Instead, each person is a composite of the different actions and reactions that come in and out of consciousness as appropriate for any given situation.

And since it is possible to know what is "on our mind" but not what is literally inside it, direct inspection of the self will probably not lead to a true picture. There is a great deal of psychological research that shows that children don't grow up directly knowing what they are thinking. Instead, they, like all of us, make a guess, in part by observing what they are doing and in part by listening to what others say about them. Adults are also rarely able, under careful questioning, to report what is going on inside. We are simply not organized for self-knowledge, no matter how much we'd like to think we are. The mental system, instead, is geared for acting, and self-observation is very difficult.

Traditions like Sufism and Christian mysticism that emphasize rigorous self-observation may have a handle on the problem. People find when they observe themselves that their reactions don't follow their preconceived ideas of who they are. They may think of themselves as orderly and serene, for example, but find, after examining their actions, that they are actually driven by excitement, that they have a constant need for stimulation, and that their emotions run the gamut from joy to despair.

The examples are endless of how heredity and environment interact to produce each unique individual. And no one, certainly not I, could put all this information together simply and easily into a "self-help" book. So don't expect to discover in these pages a formula for finding yourself. It just can't be done. Consider this: at any mating, one male and one female could produce 52 trillion biologically distinct individuals. While many of these wouldn't be genetically viable, this combination comes from just two partners. Factor in the number of different people who can meet and mate, and the aggregate becomes practically infinite. Simply put, human individuality is genetically too complex for any one system to explain. We can, however, unearth some basic dimensions on which people differ and try to offer a few clues about why we are so different from one another. To rephrase Lincoln: "You can't explain all of the people all of the time." Perchance 30 percent of the people 10 percent of the time would be a start, though.

In this book, I am not going to offer new or revised self-observation techniques, nor do I want to resuscitate any of the current systems of personality typing. In their stead, I am going to offer another approach, one that builds on the concrete observations of modern science in the areas of child development, personality testing, brain organization, and genetics. Research has provided striking new observations of how babies develop in families; an immense quantity of information has been gathered from personality testing, as well as from clinical observations; and breakthroughs in the study of the brain and of genetics shed new light on how human beings work. All of this provides a bounty of evidence on how and why we act the way we do and offers some beginning insights on the origins of the self. This evidence, developed from the "external" observations of modern science, may well provide us with a better way to observe and understand our own acts.

I am going to go on to look at why we have the attitudes toward our nature that we do. Then I will consider the beginnings of individuality—how babies differ. We find surprises in each area: blue eyes, for instance, may be more significant than other external signs, especially skin color.

The centerpiece of the book is a hypothesis that there are three main dimensions to individual differences. I've tried to base this analysis on three independent scientific realms of research. There needs be an underlying physiological mechanism that produces a difference, and there needs be a consistent psychological result in all those millions of tests we all take. And finally there needs be consistent clinical and personal evidence for the dimension. I am thus trying to connect the biological, the psychological, and the psychiatric with each other.

The first dimension, "gain," has to do with whether we experience the world as teeming with stimulation or whether excitement seems sparse and distant to us. A person's degree of gain depends on low-level brain-stem processes that amplify or silence the flow of information from the senses to the cerebral cortex. Where we stand on the "gain" continuum has a powerful influence on most of our actions. It determines whether we like our surroundings quiet or jumpin', whether we "relax" by going kayaking over rugged falls or by lying in a hammock, and even whether we like smooth or crunchy peanut butter!

The second dimension deals with how much planning and organization we use as we go through our lives. Are we highly compartmentalized, keeping feelings out of our "judgments" and planning each day with order and exactitude? Or are we free-spirited, taking things as they come, not concerned with time or order but with the immediate moment? I call this the "deliberation-liberation" dimension. Where we stand on this continuum is influenced by the activities of the frontal lobes of the cortex and the limbic system.

The third dimension, which I call the "approach-withdrawal" continuum, has to do with our basic emotional approach to life. For some, the world is forever bright and sunny, and everything is to be embraced; for others, it is a difficult, dark place, and one needs to be careful about getting involved. The "approachers," researchers have found, seem to use the left hemisphere of the brain more than the right, since the left has more to do with the positive emotions like joy and pleasure, which signal us to approach. The right hemisphere seems to be the site of the negative feelings like anger and disgust, which signal us to move away.

The three physiological systems that I've mentioned—the brain stem, the frontal lobes and limbic system, and the hemispheres—aren't, of course, all there is to the brain, the self, or the personality, but I believe that there is now enough scientific evidence to support our focusing on them for a beginning analysis.

Using the three dimensions related to these systems, we will consider whether some mental disorders might not simply consist of normal tendencies on each continuum taken to an extreme. Does meticulousness shade into obsessiveness and then develop into obsessive-compulsive disorder? Does creativity and what we call flakiness shade into schizophrenia? Does ordinary sadness lead an individual into depression? My conclusion will challenge many existing theories: I believe that the same underlying processes that produce our normal variations in self are, at their extremes, responsible for some psychoses and neuroses.

After exploring the complexities of this question I then go on to consider some of the other powerful factors in our lives: family life, skin color, handedness, sex, and the many different "talents" of mind that we inherit. One of the most striking revelations here is that families don't make us similar to one another; they actually tend to make us different. For instance, child psychologist Sandra Scarr writes, "Upper-middle-class brothers who attend the same school and whose parents take them to the same plays, sporting events, music lessons, and therapists and use similar childrearing practices on them are little more similar in personality measures than they are to working-class or farm boys, whose lives are totally different." The point here is that there are many independent forces that contribute to who we are, and none does so in a simple way.

Finally, after all this information about how we are pretty much fixed in the way we are, comes another surprise: that the brain changes all through life and that by changing our actions, we can often reprogram ourselves. Within the confines of both basic human nature and our individual nature, there remains real room for change.

There are authentic ways to understand the roots of the individual, but knowing how the roots differ doesn't tell us everything about how the mature plant will come out. In the past two decades, neuroscientists, psychologists, and psychiatrists have made great progress in identifying different brain systems that guide human actions. And they have found an abundance of evidence that individuals differ in the way they activate these different areas of their brains. Photos of positron emission tomography (PET) scans, often published in articles about schizophrenia or organic brain disorders, offer a good way to picture how this works, for the **PET** scan shows different areas of the brain lighting up and dimming as glucose is consumed.

Different areas of the brain respond to an individual's activities in the world: the frontal cortex lights up in planning; the left or the right hemisphere lights up while reading or painting; the reticular activating system (**RAS**) of the brain stem lights up when one receives sensory input, such as a sound or taste, and it sends these signals to the cortex. Individual brains vary in terms of what areas these activities arouse.[1]

Knowing something about how these areas of the brain work may well provide a more secure basis for understanding ourselves and our differences than we can gain from making personal inferences or from using other, less inclusive personality-typing systems. Indeed, from the developments in brain science of the past fifty years, the personality testing of the past one hundred, and the useful individual insights of the past one thousand, there is more to be said about human nature than could be summarized in two thousand volumes. Yet much of this research has not reached the general public, nor has it been synthesized and looked at as part of a larger whole.

Instead, the world is now inundated with recovery programs; with personality analyses; with twelve-step, two-step, and box-step tangles of dependency; and with methods of freeing the inner Sid or the financial genius or the sex goddess within all of us. And to gods and goddesses, inner children, and binding or blinding shame, I say Godspeed. They leave our story here.

But the truth is that there are no simple formulas. Human beings are so biologically complex and are born into and make their lives in such dissimilar worlds that no one book—and certainly not this one—can "fix" any one of them. Nor can this book be a final analysis. Such an enormous amount of research is going on all over the world, from Oxford to Osaka, that anybody would be silly to claim to have the last word. Yet in considering personality, temperament, and brain research from both an American and a

---

1. I don't mean to endorse **PET** scans as a "window" to the mind, but merely to use them as a metaphor. I sometimes feel the color magazines have one picture of the deep workings of the brain that they pull out every five years to illustrate **PET** scans, fast **MRI**, or any convenient technology.

European perspective, we can identify multiple sources from which our individuality grows, develops, matures, and flowers—in other words, we can begin to discover our roots.

Of course, not everyone is interested in hearing that he or she may be limited by being left-handed, or blue-eyed, or secondborn, or from a small family, or the child of a divorce. Thomas Hardy's Tess of the D'Urbervilles cried:

> What's the use of learning that I am one of a long row only—finding out that there is set down in some old book somebody just like me, and to know that I shall only act her part; making me sad, that's all. The best is not to remember that your nature and your past doings have been just like thousands' and thousands', and that your coming life and doings'll be like thousands' and thousands'.

It's more challenging, Tess. We may be initially prompted by our inherited biology, the world then goes on to fashion each of us into a unique organism. Our "doings" are never just "like thousands' and thousands'." There are many inherent ways in which we differ from one another.

Consider these two people whom I know well. Both are successful; neither ever seems to change. One person does everything quickly and in a set order all the time; his desk is neat, his briefcase has tidy compartments for home and office sets of keys, for his train timetable, office papers, and house documents. His clothes all match and are well organized. Another is forever losing his keys; his clothes, while just as expensive, are always somehow mismatched—the purple tie just doesn't make it with the blue suit—and he finds, as does the TV character Columbo, all sorts of weird things in his pockets.

As with these two, the amount of organization and planning one exercises is a fairly fixed part of an individual's nature. But human beings are actually unfinished animals, constantly in the process of change and development. At any moment, the maps of our brains may change as we learn new things and as the world changes. When we learn a new language, our brain organization changes; if we move to a new city or get married or divorced, our map changes again. We adapt, we "create ourselves anew"—but not all of ourselves all the time. For whether we now speak French, have three kids, or have become the head of the company, we will still dress meticulously or randomly—maybe Armani random, but still random.

We're contradictory, no doubt; this is why Tess's idea that our lives are fixed holds for some areas, while the self-help idea that "anyone can do anything" has some truth in other areas. The trick is to find out where each view holds and then to stop trying to change things that can't be changed and to change what we can. In other words, we have to learn to think differently about ourselves.

It's not merely a matter of having a specific genetic inheritance and growing up in one culture, for how we grow and develop is itself influenced by the world in which we grow, just as a tree will grow differently alone in a field than it would inside a crowded ravine. Human beings are born into different cultures, with different family structures, family position, social worlds, and each of these elements radically influences our development. The possibilities are literally countless.

Think of the individual as a garden. In the very beginning, as when an infant is born, the garden is capable of growing a great many different kinds of plants. Thanks to a particular soil composition (genetics), the garden may be more likely to grow some plants more successfully than others. But pretty quickly, then, the "life experience" of the garden (such as the weather it endures and the amount of care it receives) begins to select which plants take root, which are cultivated, and which are ignored. As time passes, the garden will settle into a particular pattern. Eventually, it will become more and more difficult to introduce new plants because they will find it hard to compete with those already established.

However, there is always room for some change, perhaps for the fertilization or encouragement of a flower that was not previously favored. If a section of the garden plot is damaged—say, by the weather (in the brain, this could stand for a stroke or an injury)—its growing function may, after a time, be restored. This may happen with different plants, or the roots of the plants in the damaged territory can be moved to another part of the garden to thrive again.

If, as in the garden, life experiences have a profound effect on the cultivation of the self, how can one guide one's life to enhance one's development? First, we need to know a little more

about the specifics of how brains change with experience. Contemporary neuroscientists are just beginning to peer into the complex connections among brain, behavior, and personality. The interaction begins before birth and, perhaps most surprisingly, continues throughout life.

All animals develop differently depending on the locale in which they live; all are born unfinished. While anyone can see that animals differ in temperament, aggressiveness, need for affection, and the like, human beings are the most astonishingly variable species on earth. Human life has two developmental differences from other animals: we are born much earlier in our growth cycle than are other animals—even our brains are less developed at birth—and we are born into a much greater variety of environments than are other animals. In other words, to adapt to mountain life or desert life, a country with plentiful food or one that is barren, our development selects from our inheritance those aspects of the self that will be useful in our particular world.

There is a kind of "codevelopment" that takes place, then, based on the interaction between biological inheritance and the environment in which we live. This book looks at each of the different aspects of individuality in light of this codevelopment. This will allow us to reconsider the age-old question of which influences us more—heredity or environment. Habitats as different as Calcutta and Chicago, Norway and Nigeria winnow each person's heredity and adapt that person to the world of her or his birth.

Consider the way a child develops in infancy. If a child is born blind because the retina in each eye is blocked by an opaque lens, light can still enter the retina, but the images will never be focused. What happens if you give the child a lens transplant that corrects the optical defect in the eye?

When this operation was performed on children who had been born blind and who had remained so for their first decade, everyone expected that these children would be able to see normally because now not only were their retinas and brains intact but the lenses were also restored to their normal functioning.

But what happened was this: the new eye signals that were now clearly focused on the retina annoyed the children; they perceived them as painful and dazzling. None of these children could use the new visual information. They couldn't learn to see, to

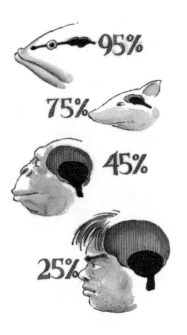

Size of adult brain at birth

process patterns, or to recognize anything. Instead of the operation giving them new life, it almost killed them. All became depressed, and some committed suicide.

The brain is incomplete without getting the general range of signals from the environment. Why should this happen? Why didn't God just wire up the brain so that it would handle any environment? Perhaps it is due to the wide variety of worlds human beings live in and the way we develop. For instance, visual systems that need to adapt to changing head size during development have to undergo constant reevaluation and change so that stability is maintained from the time of birth to time of maturity. Fixing the visual system at one specification would never work.

Sparrow songs develop with experience. Normal sparrows learn to sing in their local dialects. Sparrows from different necks of the woods have different sounds. But how do they acquire these adult song patterns? Are they innate? Do sparrows have to hear them from their parents?

The young sparrow cannot learn merely by hearing the sounds of adult sparrows alone, and it cannot learn by hearing no sounds at all. It can only learn when it is exposed to a local dialect at the right time of life. When it does, it reproduces that dialect forever without any further modification. It seems that all animals, including human beings, inherit a basic capacity for learning from a certain range of experiences, and when those experiences happen, the brain develops normally.

There is a similar critical period for language in human beings. People who change languages before six years of age seem to be able to speak their new one perfectly, while people who learn a new language after age six retain their original accent. Henry Kissinger was about six when he and his family fled Nazi Germany. Kissinger speaks English with a distinct German accent, while his younger brother speaks without one. This is not a matter of intelligence but a matter of timing. Children who suffer major brain damage to the left hemisphere when young can adapt; language moves over to the right. By age twelve or thirteen, however, this flexibility diminishes.

Understanding how impressionable development is gives us the greatest of hope for the future because it shows how we can change. I believe the implications are revolutionary.

The unfinished brain, developing after birth, wires up differently in different worlds, and this is why individuals in different cultures have such difficulty understanding each other: even their visual systems are not exactly the same. People who grow up in forests lack the depth perception that the rest of us have; those who don't inhabit the "carpentered" modern world of straight edges and lines have a different way of seeing things than those who do.

Consider these results: one group of rats was raised "normally," watching others fight and give and receive pain. In another group the rats were reared in isolation from each other. In adulthood *none of this group felt pain*, because their nervous systems never got organized to experience it.

The world has some profound effects on our development, and this fact allows us to remake ourselves through conscious choice, even in adulthood. Yet we can never abandon our inherent natures, our roots.

Part One

On Human Nature

Chapter 2

Coming of Age in Self-Understanding

The Tale of Galton, Boas, and Mead

It is one of those perennial questions.

From the time of the ancient Egyptian civilization and probably before, people have wondered whether human beings are completely determined by their innate biology or whether their environment establishes how they will be. If our parents have hot tempers, will we? If they are highly intellectual, do we have a leg up on getting a Nobel prize? Will a mother's athletic ability be passed to her son? On the other side, we wonder how far our society programs us. If I'm Italian, will I automatically enjoy life? If I'm from Finland, does it follow that I will be suicidal? Can we break free of culture? Can we break free of biology? Can we improve ourselves through cultural change? If so, is biology insignificant?

In reviewing the history of scientific efforts to determine whether individuality is governed by culture or biology, I've been very surprised by how simpleminded the "nature-versus-nurture" controversy is. Scientific ideas have shuttled back and forth between radical environmental program or one for genetic improvement, and then back and forth again. Looking at the zigzags our forbears have done may allow us to get some distance from the old either-or ideas. In truth, like sunlight on the garden, they aren't separated.

The question of the nature of human nature was much more of a concern throughout the past century; the debate was more like a series of violent conflicts, one of which we follow here.

The Nature/Nurture Meander

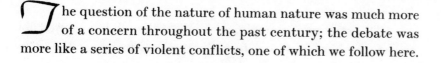

Most of us grew up in an era of post–World War II optimism, when new rights and opportunities have been extended to the previously underprivileged. Central, currently, to social progress is a view that nurture, or environment, is of foremost importance in providing people with a better life, and we thus support remedial education for the disadvantaged. All such compensatory programs are certainly important. But the unspoken assumption here is that biology isn't so important and that anyone who thinks it is is somehow opposed to social justice and progress, consciously or not. We shall see that this is not the case.

Americans have been educated to believe that all people are created equal; we assume that the ways in which we differ are due to culture. Thus, throughout most of the twentieth century, the peculiarities of different cultures and different experiences have received lots of scientific attention. Psychologists, anthropologists, educators, and psychoanalysts have all sought out the unusual and exotic in order to demonstrate the tremendous influence of culture.

Anthropologists, for example, are interested in such cultural rites as the annual festival of the Wodabe, when they adorn their skin to attract "extra women," because rituals like these show how malleable human beings' sexual attitudes are. Cultures such the Wodabe or the !Kung San, both of which are untouched by modern influences, spotlight how *different* other cultures are and how different our lives would be were we living elsewhere. Yet most of this exoticism ignores the vast amount that all humans have in common.

This view of infinite singularity was stimulated in the seventeenth century. John Locke, David Hume, and John Stuart Mill, who have been influential in forming science's view of the mind, believed that all knowledge comes from experience. The key assumption is that the mind is without any ideas or inherent tendencies other than those that arise from the world in which a person lives. This view has a long history, and while it suits some political agendas well (it is a useful argument in favor of social programs that seek to achieve equality), it must pass the test of truth. It doesn't.

This stream of thought, influential though it was, was not to last. The blow first came from Charles Darwin, who in the 1850s showed that human beings had evolved along with the rest of life on earth and were descended from a common ancestor. Darwin proposed the theory of natural selection, and this theory, combined with modern genetics, forms the basis of the modern theory of evolution, the accepted explanation of how organisms change through time. One consequence of evolutionary thinking was the idea that far from being unlimited in abilities, human beings, like other animals, are biologically adapted to their environment. Thus many reactions to the world are already present at birth and the mind is not a blank slate.

*D*arwin's cousin, Frances Galton, picked up the ball and ran with it, setting the course for the modern age of genetic determinism. A Fellow of the Royal Society and honorary secretary general of the Royal Geographical Society, Galton was interested in the "human side of geography." When he read *On the Origin of Species,* he absorbed it immediately and thought of Darwin's work "in the same way converts from barbarism think of the teacher who first relieved them from the intolerable burden of their superstition."

If organisms develop through random "natural" selection, why, Galton believed, should not human beings intervene and apply deliberate selection to our own species in order to improve our mental and physical attributes? After all, this is how new breeds of animals come into being all the time, under the watchful care of animal husbandry. Similar actions would liberate humanity.

Thus arose the wider field of eugenics, from the Greek for "good birth." While today it seems brutal, Galton's eugenics had the goal of improving society at its core by changing its composition. It was called "hereditary improvement," a program in which, Galton hoped, "a perfect enthusiasm for improving the race might develop itself among the educated classes," who would consider it their "paramount duty, to anticipate the slow and stubborn processes of natural selection, by endeavoring to breed out feeble constitutions and petty and ignoble instincts, and to breed in those which are vigorous and noble and social."

For some it would make a fun program, for eugenecists believed that extra reproduction among the already educated would "improve the breed" by increasing the number of genetically superior, industrious smarties. Sounds archaic? The same thing is going on today in Singapore, where a somewhat paternalistic but purposeful government provides workaholic, nonreproductive yuppies with their own special romantic cruises and dating agencies to reverse the trend of lower rates of childbirth with increasing levels of education. This amounts to saying, "Lie back and think of improving the country." And, of course, in Galton's plan, the lower classes also somehow had to be discouraged in their voracious animal couplings, lest they become too numerous.

A boost to Galton's cause came in 1900 with the resurgent interest in genetics. From then on, putting his plans for a eugenic revolution into action became a self-confessed "crusade." Darwin himself, whose work had provided the springboard for Galton's model of "race improvement," did not support the idea (although he called Galton's book *Hereditary Genius* "interesting and original"). For although Darwin thought that natural selection was of essential significance in human history, he did not altogether discount the contributions of cultural factors to human nature. He ends his *Descent of Man* with the observation that moral qualities are developed through learning and are not simply inherited.

The University of London formally acknowledged eugenics in 1905, and the Eugenics Education Society was created in 1907 to speed the credo. Eugenics became increasingly popular in both England and the United States. Stanford's former president David Starr Jordan chaired the American Breeders Association Committee on Eugenics, whose goal it was to research human heredity and to "emphasize the value of superior blood and the menace to society of inferior blood." The enthusiasm for breeding, however, also bred overenthusiastic notions. In 1910, in *Eugenics: The Science of Human Improvement by Better Breeding*, Charles B. Davenport wrote of the necessity to "annihilate the hideous serpent of hopelessly vicious protoplasm."

In Galton's thinking, the distinctions between individuals observed in different societies were the result of their having different genetic legacies. This line of thought led to a scientific racism, where "civilized" and "uncivilized" societies were thought to be marked by different degrees of genetic fitness, inborn character traits, and intellectual abilities. White Americans "bred from the most restless and combative class of Europe" were therefore genetically destined to be "enterprising" and "impatient" but also "furious," "tolerant of violence," and the like. Blacks fared much worse. And you can guess how well Englishmen came out.

*E*ugenics thrived just before World War I, when modern biology seemed to promise humanity a way to control its composition and destiny. Heady days. This emphasis on "nature, not nurture" was to last until the anthropologists' revolt. Franz Boas was among those who opposed the extremist views of Galton. "Genetic determinism" provoked Boas to formalize the competing "cultural determinism" in the 1910s and 1920s. For the next two decades, the outspoken Boas rose to fame as he held that the laws of biology did not figure into the story of human nature *at all*. Social processes, in his view, were completely isolated from organic ones, and there was no "bridge" connecting the two.

The eugenics movement continued to be a formidable adversary, and in 1918 the Galton Society was formed in the United States. The debate grew hotter when the behaviorists, who were the heirs to Locke and the empiricists and who rejected the influence of "instinct," took the side of Boas. Since knowledge comes only from experience, they argued, people can better themselves by altering their environment.

Philosophers, sociologists, and social psychologists also fell in line with Boas. Instead of controlling nature, the goal should be to control nurture in order to improve the race. B. F. Skinner's *Walden 2,* for example, proposed a society regulated by a system of rewards. Advocates of "nurture" were fueled by an opposition to the racism inherent in eugenics. And in hindsight—before Hitler and Milosevic—how benign this controversy seems.[1]

I'm sure that these various opinions were only made more fervent by the kind of obstinate folly that often takes hold in

---

1. The terms used by the eugenicists still linger in the minds of many. While writing this book, I picked up the February 9, 1993, issue of *PC* magazine to find one of my favorite columnists discussing a ranking of products: "If you think about it, the concept and term *best of breed* makes you cringe. . . . For one thing, when I think of best of breed I think of dogs! Or Nazis!"

academia. We are taught that science progresses through the testing of opposing views and that a crucial experiment can obliterate other viewpoints. One party says that something is all white, the other all black, and they then amass evidence supporting their viewpoints. They may search out black flecks in a particular stone and claim it represents the whole, only to be "refuted" by others who point to the flecks of white.

The behaviorists' rejection of "instinct" was mirrored by early twentieth-century brain scientists who considered the brain almost blank. Perhaps because of the difficulties of research on the human brain, these scientists' ignorance and their ideology led them to think of the brain as unspecialized and undifferentiated, a single mass, perhaps a pinkish Jell-O that could become anything with learning.

Of course, this was before the discovery of the single neuron, which gave rise to an intermediate position: that while there *are* different components in the brain, the mass *as a whole* is a blank slate. Increasing understanding of the structure of the brain made this view as palatable as Jell-O mold with bits of fruit cocktail in it.

The concept of the brain as a blank slate supported the hopeful approach taken by American education. But while the social aims of equality of opportunity are quite laudable, the idea of equality of ability was mistaken, as we will see throughout this book. The argument between all black or all white, all social dynamics or all innate biology was really just so much scientific trash, since there was no evidence to support either viewpoint.

Margaret Mead, Sex, and Temperament in the South Seas

*I*nto the midst of this controversy came the woman who was to change society's view of human individuality for most of the twentieth century. Margaret Mead's research in eastern Samoa and her 1929 book *Coming of Age in Samoa* set the tone for the next fifty years. Boas was frustrated by the need to demonstrate the impact of different cultural practices on individuals. One way to prove his point was to consider a "fact of life" in America and to show that it was not a factor in other cultures. Adolescence in America was fraught with storm and stress, sexual repression and deviousness. If a tribe could be found that didn't have such tribu-lation, then upbringing, rather than human nature, would have to be the reason!

In Mead, Boas found the talented young doctoral student he needed to undertake this study. She began her graduate studies in 1923 and became interested in field study on cultural change in Polynesia. Boas enlisted her for a study of adolescence among girls in a non-Western society. He had originally decided on an American Indian tribe for this study, but Mead, whose interest had already focused on Polynesia, wanted the South Seas. They compromised on Samoa.

Mead spent nine months from 1925 to 1926 studying female adolescence on Ta'u, a small island in the Manu'an archipelago, which had been under American control for twenty-one years. The Manu'ans had lived as converted Protestants for about eighty years. Mead lived in the home of an American family.

In *Coming of Age in Samoa*, Mead portrayed life there as "characterized by ease":

> Samoa is a place where no one plays for very high stakes, no one pays very high prices, no one suffers for his convictions or fights to the death for special ends. Disagreements between parent and child are settled by the child's moving across the street, between a man and his village by the man's removal to the next village, between a husband and his wife's seducer by a few fine mats.

"Coming of age" referred to the stormy time of puberty and adolescence—stormy to us Americans, anyway. Not so in Samoa! There, according to Mead, adolescence was a dreamy and uncom-plicated time because Samoans were raised in a society with "few situations for conflict," where family life involved no troublesome bonds or imposition of guilt feelings, and where sexual contact was "the pastime *par excellence*." This book made an exciting read even decades later when I was in college, at a time when everyone was rebelling against the strictness of American culture, and it must have been doubly exciting in the thirties. Mead's phrase *pas-time par excellence* offered a very attractive way to discuss certain actions during that period of my life.

Mead portrayed a culture extremely permissive in sexual re-lations; where premarital sex was unhindered and adolescent girls delayed marriage "through as many years of casual lovemaking as possible." She wrote that "love between the sexes is a light and pleasant dance." There were specific initiation rites, well-ordered systems of trysts in her sexual South Sea paradise, so unlike the coming of age in our society. "Nurture" above all could change this most basic and important human behavior. Thus questions of a "basic nature" were sidelined, since culture could override nature. No one had a fixed predestination; what we will become depends on our culture.

Derek Freeman, however, upon whose account of Mead, Boas, and Galton I am basing this discussion, visited Samoa in the sixties and seventies and found a very different picture. Mead had described adultery as "not regarded as very serious," adding that "jealousy, as a widespread phenomenon," was "very rare in Samoa." But Freeman found that adultery was listed as an offense in the Regulations and Orders for the Government of American Samoa during Mead's time. And in the local police records, there were plenty of violent incidents that were the result of the sexual jealousy of both males and females.

Mead had described Samoan male sexuality as nonaggressive in comparison to the Western and wrote that "the idea of forcible rape or of any sexual act to which both participants do not give themselves freely is completely foreign to the Samoan mind." But Freeman found that Samoa has and has had among the highest rates of rape in the world. This is partly due to the cultural preoccupation among Samoan men with stealing a woman's virginity, as I discuss in the Notes at the end of this book.

The high incidence of rape was reported by missionaries as early as 1845 and by the police of Western Samoa in contemporary times. At the time that Mead was pursuing her research, rape was the third most prevalent crime in Samoa, after assault and theft.

Described by Mead as "the age of maximum ease," adolescence in Samoa was supposedly exempt from the storm and stress that plagues "young people in more complex—and often also more primitive—societies."

In doing his research in Samoa in the sixties, Freeman was told about the adolescent experience by both male and female adolescents and well-educated former adolescents. *All* described stressful relations with parents, the constant threat of violence, and anger at figures of authority. Most rebellious gestures happened around age sixteen, especially among boys. Similarly, adolescent girls indulged in verbal aggression with particularly high frequency, probably as a result of peer-group conflicts.

How do we reconcile these two conflicting reports? The truth is that Boas needed a central example of how culture could change human nature completely. And he got it and delivered it to us, and we read and reread it generation after generation. And it got into the literature because Boas, in his eagerness to refute the arguments of the eugenecists, did not follow the usual scientific procedures and rushed Mead's results into the literature; Mead, meanwhile, had seen only what she was sent to see.

In the more than fifty years since Mead published her conclusions, there has been a swing back toward an appreciation of the role of biology in our individuality. That human beings evolved and come into the world with the "seeds" of a number of abilities, from color vision to emotions to language, is now well accepted in the sciences.

The "absolute cultural determinism" championed by Boas and Mead could not withstand the impact of science's increased understanding of the evolution and function of the brain, the discovery of DNA, and the evidence concerning the role of genetics in behavior. Now, with a better appreciation of our neural apparatus and the basic "programs" with which human beings are furnished when we enter the world, most scientists view the environment as a kind of system of selection, operating more like a gardener rather than as an exclusive force.

On the other hand, biologists now also give more credence to culture. Boas and his followers did succeed in getting the scientific world to take seriously the implications and dynamics of cultural influence.

Thus, the resolution of this long-standing argument unites culture and biology, and while the world develops the individual, it can only develop what is already there. At birth, human beings have many innate predispositions, yet we are born unfinished, open to development. While all of us speak language, the particular language, including the accent, varies by region. Our locale gives us our final "finishing." Individuals need the world to give them their individuality, yet the world can only develop what we've inherited.

Chapter 3

From the Cell to the Self

You are your parents' donation to human evolution. You can probably see much of them in your looks and bearing. The common human heritage is multifold. We each develop a large brain, erect posture, color vision. But each human being is also one of a kind—at once like all others and yet like no other person who has ever lived.

Some of our individual attributes are obvious: specific physical traits, such as sex and eye color, are set at conception and almost completely unaffected by the normal range of life experiences. However, there is also a more subtle inheritance that consists of dispositions toward tallness, or toward diabetes or schizophrenia, or even toward certain interests and attitudes. And there is an inheritance of temperament characteristics, such as our quickness, our emotional tone, and our type of cerebration.

The single cell that matures into the human form does so in a precise way, governed by patterns set by genetic inheritance through the millennia. The brain, once an undifferentiated part of that single cell, emerges as an organ so complex that no computer, no matter how large, can mimic its function.

The cell also contains the specifications for the design and construction of the nervous system and the senses, sensors (and censors) so intricate that they select only one-trillionth of the information reaching them that is relevant for survival. The neural network analyzes these outside signals, sending them along to the higher functions of the brain. This entire process is part of our genetic endowment.

In this chapter, we will consider many of the questions about our evolution, about where we come from and what we may

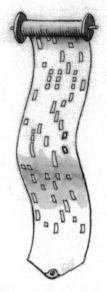

The roll of inheritance

become. How much does the genetic code specify? Most behavior is the product of genes plus experiences, just as a tree grows partly from its nature, partly from the rain and the site in which it sits. Some human behaviors may be more determined by nature, some by nurture, but all are shaped by differing combinations of both.

This fact allows the nature-nurture argument to survive in a new form. While most of us now accept that there is some biological basis for different behaviors, there is great controversy over just how much is specified in the genes and how far conscious influence can pull us away from our heritage.

Each person is dealt a complex genetic hand at birth, a set of biological instructions for fabricating a human body and brain. The gene, which is the basic component of heredity in all living things, is made of **DNA** (deoxyribonucleic acid). DNA is contained in the nucleus of every living cell. The **DNA** molecule looks like a twisted ladder. The rungs hold four chemical "bases"—adenine, thymine, guanine, and cytosine.

All life's blueprints for growth and development come from these bases. What differs between organisms, even between you and an amoeba, is only the arrangement of the four bases along the double helix of the DNA molecule. In ordinary life, we exaggerate our differences. How different do you think someone would be who had just 6 percent of his or her genes differing from yours? French? Aboriginal? No, a 6 percent difference in your genetic arrangement and you would be a rhesus monkey. Chimpanzees differ from us about 2 percent. The average unrelated strangers differ by approximately a tenth of 1 percent.

A gene is a segment of **DNA** that encodes a specific characteristic. Each human being has twenty-three pairs of chromosomes that together hold approximately fifty thousand genes, which are arranged like beads on a string. One of each pair of chromosomes, such as for eye color, comes from each parent. When the mother's ovum or the father's sperm is formed, the pair of genes is split. Then a new pair can form when egg and sperm join in the conception of a child.

The chromosomes of pair twenty-three determine an individual's sex. The sex chromosomes have two different shapes: one

WOLF MONKEY

WOLFGANG AMADEUS MOZART

2%

looks like an X, the other like a Y. A female has two X chromosomes in pair twenty-three, while a male has one X and one Y chromosome. Thus, because he can contribute either kind of chromosome, the sex of a child is always determined by the father's sperm: if he contributes the X chromosome, the child will be a girl; if he contributes the Y chromosome, the child will be a boy.

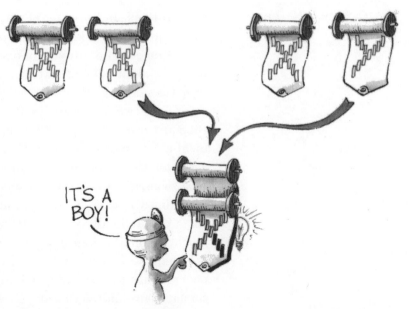

IT'S A BOY!

And there are sex differences even in the womb. One might assume that the chance of conceiving a male or female is fifty-fifty, but this is not so. For every 100 females, 140 males are conceived. Sperm carrying Y chromosomes may be more mobile than those carrying X chromosomes and so may reach the egg first. Interestingly, it seems that males are more "expendable." They are more fragile, too: of the 140 conceived, only 105 boys are born for every 100 girls. The XY (male) unit is more frail than the XX unit in the womb. This fragility continues: more males than females die at every age level in infancy, childhood, and adulthood—until there are so few males left that the death rate is higher for females. Thus, women typically live longer than men, and there are more females than males.

The only exception to the rule of genetic uniqueness is identical twins. Identical twins are monozygotic—they develop from the same fertilized egg. Fraternal twins develop when the mother releases two eggs and each is fertilized by different sperms. They are no more alike than any two siblings. Genetic similarity is important in tracing the role of genetic factors in individuality. Because identical twins offer the only possible instance of identical heredity, they are prized for studies, and many of the studies we'll consider use them.

Next most similar in genetic makeup are siblings, who share many of the same genes from their parents. There is some degree of genetic similarity among all relatives: parents, aunts, uncles, half-brothers, and so on. Whenever we speak of "blood relatives," we are actually speaking about people with a genetic similarity.

Studies of inheritance of one characteristic or another often compare identical and fraternal twins. As identical twins come from the same egg, they share all their genes, while fraternal twins come from two separate eggs and so are no more alike genetically than any other siblings. If heredity is important in the development of any particular trait, from depression to spatial ability to eye color, the fraternal twins will be more different than the identical twins; if the hereditary element is unimportant, then fraternal twins will share as great a similarity as the identical twins.

Adopted children are often studied in order to show how much the family environment, as opposed to heredity, influences one characteristic or another. If a trait is inherited, we would expect siblings who are adopted into different families to be more similar than children who are unrelated but adopted into the same family. If, however, heredity plays no real part in the development of the trait, then siblings who are adopted apart will not resemble each other in the trait, and unrelated children adopted together will be no more different than actual siblings.

Some inherited traits such as myopia (nearsightedness) may not show up right away. Eye color is determined by one gene or, at the most, a few genes, but most human traits are determined by a combination of many. It is possible for a child to have nostrils like the mother's and the bridge of the nose like the father's. Some characteristics are so likely to be inherited that they come to characterize a family: for instance, the Hapsburgs, the ruling family of the Holy Roman Empire for generations, had a characteristic protruding lip. Some inherited characteristics are rather inconsequential: whether you have attached or detached earlobes, for example, whether or not you can roll your tongue, or whether your second toe is longer than your big toe.

We are certainly dealt a hand at birth, but how we play the hand is also important. Genes may predispose an individual to certain traits, but how that predisposition develops depends on experience. For these characteristics, the genes govern the "range of reaction." Height, for instance, may be influenced by environment in the form of nutrition. A genetic predisposition for a disease may or may not express itself, depending on such specific experiences as diet, stress, and culture.

Every organism, even the simplest bacterium, contains more genetic potential than can be "expressed," that is, than can appear in the living organism. The expression depends on circumstances and opportunity. For example, Caucasians are generally taller than Orientals because the genetic potential for height in the Caucasian gene pool produces taller people. However, with improved nutrition, Japanese people brought up in North America have grown taller than their compatriots in Japan. They express the upper range of their height potential.

Now those in Japan are growing taller, too. Do you recall the pocket-size Japanese cars of the sixties? They were so in part because the Japanese people were small. Now that the Japanese people are larger, their cars have grown as well. The current Toyota Corolla is 20 percent larger than the same model in the sixties, and the Japanese now make big cars like the Lexus.

Comparing Heredity and Environment

*I*t is easy to analyze the comparative contributions of heredity and environment in a physical trait such as height. The roots of mental abilities like intelligence or of disabilities are much more difficult to sort out.

Schizophrenia, which affects about 1 percent of the population, has genetic as well as social causes. The genetic contribution was discovered by examining the family histories of schizophrenics and comparing them with those of nonschizophrenics. This study revealed a greater occurrence of schizophrenia within the schizophrenic's families than among the families of nonschizophrenics.

Within schizophrenic families, the greater the genetic similarity, the greater the incidence of schizophrenia. The identical twin of a schizophrenic is more likely to suffer from the disorder than is a fraternal twin. Similarly, a sibling of a schizophrenic has a greater chance of being one than does a cousin, and the child of a schizophrenic has twelve to thirteen times the average chance of being a schizophrenic. This is a predisposition only; in a favorable and healthy environment, the serious disorder of schizophrenia stands less of a chance of being expressed.

Ethology—the study of animal behavior under natural conditions—has contributed many studies that shed light on the relative influence of genetics versus that of environment. For instance, when a newly hatched duckling is from twelve to eighteen hours old, something quite remarkable happens: if it recognizes something moving and it follows that movement for ten minutes, then that object will become "imprinted" on the duckling, and it will continue to follow the object anywhere.

In nature, of course, a baby duckling is most likely to see its mother during its first hours, so this reaction evolved to help the animal survive. Such reactions are thus called evolutionarily stable strategies (ESS); following them leads to a greater chance of reproductive success. However, during those crucial hours, if a scientist intervenes and shows the duckling a rectangle or a decoy on wheels, it will follow that object instead. In the most dramatic demonstration, Konrad Lorenz, one of the most influential ethologists, himself appeared in front of goslings at the right time. The tiny goslings followed him as if he were their mother and cried when he was not around.

The neural program for imprinting is simple: all that seems necessary are instructions analogous to "follow anything that appears within twelve to eighteen hours after you are hatched." Many analyses show that behaviors as complex as courting and the tendency to avoid incest are similarly prompted.

Many evolutionarily stable strategies appear in childrearing, since this activity is too important to be left to finicky individual choices. What if the mother doesn't like the child? Many innate reactions of the child, such as distress calls (crying), stimulate innate reactions in the mother (the desire to feed, clean, or soothe the baby). These reactions occur whether the mother likes her child or not. In addition, a network of attachments persists between mothers (or other caregivers) and their offspring.

Our Common Inheritance

Human beings share a common inheritance and many physical, behavioral, and mental characteristics that set us off from other animals. For example, we're *bipedal*—that is, we walk on two feet instead of all four. And because our forelimbs are free from weight-bearing responsibilities, we can use tools.

Also because of the pelvis necessary to support our erect posture, our birth process is difficult, and we are born earlier in our development than other animals. Thus, the majority of the brain's development occurs outside the womb, exposed to and influenced by many different environments, events, and people. And because the environment is different for each person, the specific abilities that each of us develops differ considerably.

The newborn of most other species can fend for itself within a relatively short time, so the mother can almost immediately resume her place in the group while still providing her young with food and protection. But taking care of a human infant is a full-time job. The father-mother-child unit "bonds" into a family unit that is typical of our species.

We share more than that: we all begin life with the same basic emotions, the same color vision, the same time orientation. We are more similar to each other than we think. Anthropologist Don Brown has described in great detail the common characteristics of individuals in societies throughout the world. He calls these characteristics the traits of the "Universal People" (UP).

The UP have their cultural knowledge embedded in a language, which has a grammar and a set of phonemes. They speak in abstractions. Their phonemes are produced and channeled through the oral and nasal cavities. Their language allows them to think and speak in abstractions. They also lie and have symbolic speech. And they manage to express much more than their words indicate through nonverbal gestures, all of which are similar around the world.

The Universal People have many complex terms for relatives, using separate terms for different kin categories. They are deeply concerned with kinship. Kinships are translatable to the relationships that exist at procreation, mother, father, son, and daughter. They have separate terminologies for age and for status, as well.

They are both excited and repelled by sexual attention. They have many elaborate rituals to govern sexual acts. There are standards for genital modesty. In almost all societies, people do not make love nor do they urinate or defecate in public.

The Universal People live part, if not all, of their lives in groups. They recognize social identities, such as cousin, chieftain, mistress. Their most important but not their only group is the biological family. There is always an organized system for bringing up children.

They have childhood fears; they have attachments. They recognize individuals by faces. They have shelter. They know how to use fire even if they don't know how to make it.

They use the same basic emotions and communicate mostly via facial expressions and tone of voice. They make tools and use them cooperatively, and they also cooperate in family raising, unlike almost all species, and in food gathering and preparation. When their cooperation breaks down, there are sets of regulations and procedures that provide a means of conflict resolution, from primitive tribal councils to the United Nations.

They have rituals for a spiritual life and a set of beliefs to explain the mysterious. They have myths and an idea about the world in which they live. They might have poetry. And they dance.

However, with all this in common, each human being isn't "created equal" to others on almost any dimension, from height, to weight, to skin color, to eye color. Many thinkers have confused the desire to improve the lot of people through giving them equality of opportunity with the idea that people are the same. Offering compensation for deficiencies is one thing, but assuming that we are biologically identical is a myth that destroys.

Thus, we human beings inherit a set of abilities that form a common ground. Yet the inheritance is so complex that it is not exactly the same in each of us. So while there are universals, each of us has a slightly different dowry. In one person, emotions are strong, language abilities not so; in another, movement skills are greater than language skills; in a third, language is paramount. These are the roots we are following, the roots of individuality, of our selves.

Part Two

Forms of Temperament

Chapter 4

Early Differences

We all inherit the predispositions of the Universal People (UP), but this inheritance isn't completely equal. Each of us gets our abilities in slightly different measure. Even though we all partake of the faculties of language and of color vision and of the abilities to write and to make music, it is obvious that individuals differ in the degree to which they possess these talents, as well as in the way they act. Some inherited elements are quite specific, and it can take an unusual situation to discover them.

Twin girls were separated in infancy and raised apart by different adoptive parents. Unlike fraternal twins, these girls were monozygotic; that is, identical, conceived from a single egg of the mother and sperm of the father. Each one was the other's genetic duplicate.

When the twins were two and a half years old, the adoptive mother of the first girl was asked a variety of questions. Everything was fine with Shauna, she indicated, except for her eating habits. "The girl is impossible. Won't touch anything I give her. No mashed potatoes, no bananas, nothing without cinnamon. Everything has to have cinnamon on it. I'm really at my wit's end with her about this. We fight at every meal. She wants cinnamon on everything!"

Experiences play a role
in our development
(character is the whetherman)

In the house of the second twin, far away from the first, no eating problem was mentioned at all by the other mother. "Ellen eats well," she said, adding after a moment: "As a matter of fact, as long as I put cinnamon on her food she'll eat anything."

PETER AND ALEXANDER NEUBAUER, *NATURE'S THUMBPRINT*

Our individuality, from the general, such as how active we are, to the specific, such as whether we want cinnamon on our food or how we sing a specific note, has its source right at the beginning moment of our conception. Here's how Aldous Huxley put it in his "Fifth Philosopher's Song":

A million, million spermatozoa,
All of them alive,
Out of their cataclysm but one poor Noah
Dare hope to survive
And among that billion minus one
Might have chanced to be
Shakespeare, another Newton, a new Donne,
But the One was me.

During the nine months following the beginning moment, the fertilized cell divides again and again, forming the brain, all the internal organs, the muscles, skin, and bones of a human being. There are three distinct periods in utero: the germinal period, the embryonic period, and the fetal period. The germinal period begins at the moment of fertilization and ends about a week later when the fertilized egg, repeatedly dividing, has moved down the fallopian tube and implanted itself in the uterus. The embryonic period lasts from implantation until about the eighth week of pregnancy. This is the critical stage of development for the nervous system. In about the ninth week, the fetal period begins with the baby's first independent reaction to the world: the fetus responds to upsets by flexing its torso and extending its head.

Outside influences can affect fetal development and thus have an impact on the individual that fetus will become. Some events, like maternal stress or drug taking, may harm the fetus. Nutrition in utero is so important that it can affect the whole of the individual's life; effects can be found in intelligence as well as in health and longevity. It is quite easy to tell if a middle-aged man is likely to have a heart attack; just find out how much he weighed at birth. According to a set of fascinating new findings from Southampton in England:

> A person's weight at birth is a better indicator of their chances of CHD (coronary heart disease) than their cholesterol levels. We are not saying that smoking and the rest are irrelevant but birth weight seems more important, and the bigger the baby the lower the risk.

> CAROLINE FALL

There are complete birth records in Hertfordshire and Preston in England that go back to the 1920s and that provide infant mortality figures and the weight at birth and at one year for the survivors. Low birth weight (LBW)[1] was related to the risk of a stroke later in life, while low weight up to a year after birth was associated with chronic bronchitis. Heart disease was linked to low weight at both times. Low birth weight has long been an indicator of problems for the child, but until recently it had not been linked to problems for the adult.

Three towns in the north of England are about equal in income and life-style, but seventy years ago one was infamously poor, another was average, and the third was affluent. The pattern of deaths today reflect not the situation at present or how many have given up smoking or cut out fat in the last five years but rather the conditions seventy or eighty years ago, when poverty led to low-birth-weight babies. The previously poor town with LBW babies seventy years ago has higher rates of heart disease now than those more affluent towns with more normal weight babies.

There are also, of course, beneficial influences in the womb. The fetus hears muffled speech after six months of gestation and is attuned to rhythm and melody. In one study, expectant mothers hummed "Mary Had a Little Lamb" three times a day during

---

1. LBW is defined as less than 5.5 pounds and refers both to preterm (premature) babies (thirty-seven weeks or less gestation) and small-for-date (SFD) babies, defined as two standard deviations below average. When babies are small for their date of birth, it is usually due to some intrauterine retardation. Seventy-five percent of all LBW babies result from prematurity, and 25 percent are SFD. In the United States, 7.6 percent of all babies are LBW; in the United Kingdom, 6.5 percent are LBW. Causes include a family tendency to prematurity, mothers who are unusually young or old, and socioeconomic factors.

pregnancy; their babies, after birth, were more likely to be calmed by the tune when they cried. Scientists have also observed prenatal responses to touch and light.

Although babies are helpless, the seeds of adult abilities are present from the beginning. Those seeds begin to sprout and bear fruit: a helpless baby blossoms into an adult capable of an extraordinary range of motor abilities, from running to writing. Mentally, a newborn, who can only recognize its mother's odor and face and can barely track a moving light, blooms into an adult who can imagine and invent things never before dreamed of.

This development is necessary, since when babies are born, they face new experiences such as sounds, hot and cold temperatures, movements, and pain. But they are prepared! While their actions might seem a bit uncoordinated to an adult, newborns are organized. It's true that they don't have the full complement of the Universal People's abilities early on, but they don't really need to know much about settling tribal disputes at their age.

What they have is the set of abilities and reactions that belong to what might be called the Universal Baby (UB). Only two hours after birth, for example, newborns can follow a slowly moving light in front of their eyes. If a nipple or a finger is put into their mouths, they begin to suck on it. This sucking response is very strong, because sucking is the only way for them to obtain food. If you gently stroke their cheeks or the corner of their mouths, they will turn their heads in that direction; this is called "rooting," and it is an attempt to find their mother's nipple. In addition, from birth, babies are attracted to faces, which is useful because being close to other people is vital to babies' survival.

Many innate movements of infants are the building blocks of such sophisticated skills as walking and talking. The spontaneous lip movements of newborns are the same as those used in adult speech. In the first few months of life, an infant makes most of the sounds of every known language. Japanese toddlers have no trouble distinguishing L's and R's, but later on they lose this ability. An English-speaking friend of mine who grew up in South Africa told me that when her child was a toddler, she was drinking coffee with some friends who spoke !Xosa, the language that involves distinctive clicks. They were kidding my friend about her inability to make this sound and were having a good time producing it for her. She couldn't do it, but all of a sudden her child began to produce the sound! He obviously hadn't lost the ability yet.

Babies' Individuality

*A*long with all that they have in common, infants also show unique individual traits. Some are more active than others, some are more sociable, some more interested in the world around them. It is from these seeds that the adult grows. Infants early on show consistent differences in friendliness and anxiety level, which form part of their early character. There are interesting differences between shy and uninhibited children. Many two-year-old children avoid much contact, are extremely shy with strangers and timid in unfamiliar situations. Others seem quite sociable, outgoing, and spontaneous and can be fearless in approaching unfamiliar people and events.

As part of the UB inheritance, newborns already have an approach-withdrawal system: they turn toward interesting noises and away from unpleasant events. Yet the tendencies to approach or withdraw from events are very different in different babies. Some have a strong attraction response to events outside of themselves; others seem self-contained. Some children are outgoing and expressive; some also cry a lot. A baby's cry gets the attention of the caregiver, usually the mother, who tries to comfort him or her, so an expressive baby may obtain food and the comfort of caregivers better than a quieter one. Babies also have characteristic emotions: some seem always glum, while others smile often. Of course, every baby does everything, yet the relative amount of smiling and scowling is certainly a characteristic of the child.

The limbic system is the part of the brain that generates emotionality and other drives, and children of different temperaments display distinctive physiological characteristics that imply different innate thresholds in the limbic system to novel and challenging events. Some children respond with fright to minor upsets, others ignore major challenges. Both shy and outgoing children seem to stay the same way from birth until at least their eighth birthday. Probably they stay that way all their lives, but we do not yet know for sure, since this research, headed by Jerome Kagan of Harvard, will take a lifetime!

The strength of the "amplification" (how strongly one experiences a given sound or light) in the nervous system to outside events seems a basic characteristic of the infant, and this characteristic remains with us for life. This was determined by giving babies lemon juice to taste—a surprisingly easy way to determine some basic differences in the way people respond to the world. Sour and bitter tastes activate heart rate. Infants whose heart rate greatly increases in response to the juice are likely to act in an inhibited manner, because they have a higher level of amplification in their brain circuits than do children with lower heart-rate responses. I'll explain this seeming paradox—that high amplification leads to inhibition—in a moment and then treat it more extensively in Chapter Six.

As any mother knows, babies show strong temperamental variation early on, and it's important to understand that individuals seem to be born with fundamentally different reactions. Again, children with high heart rates remain unusually inhibited throughout this period.

A high level of norepinephrine (adrenaline), which is often associated with the high arousal I've just described, is associated with shyness, low sensory thresholds—and blue eyes. Jerome Kagan reports that blue-eyed children between two and eight years of age are more shy than brown-eyed ones. Why would this be true? Kagan posits that the high levels of norepinephrine (adrenaline) in inhibited children during prenatal and postnatal life could be responsible. Norepinephrine can inhibit the production of melanin (the pigment that causes eye color) in the melanocytes, the cells that produce and hold pigment in the iris.

Now, these higher levels of norepinephrine could be due to direct genetic influences or to stress-related activities. However, it is more likely that there is a genetic link, as yet undiscovered, between high adrenaline level and blue eyes.

If shy children do produce more norepinephrine when stimulated, it means that they mobilize internally to stimulation more strongly than do uninhibited children. This explains why they are largely quiet and timid, although this explanation may not be obvious at first. Norepinephrine lowers the threshold of reaction in the amygdala; thus, children with higher levels of norepinephrine will have greater sympathetic reactivity. Therefore, there is probably an association between norepinephrine levels and the high-arousal characteristic of introversion, which is probably linked to shyness as well.

A study by Richard Davidson and Jerome Kagan shows that infants who differ in whether they move toward the world or shrink from it differ in the way they activate their two cerebral hemispheres. This has been found very early on in life. If there are fundamental brain differences at birth, these might help explain some variations in temperament that blossom later in life. We shall have more to say about this in the next few chapters.

These seeds of early differences bear fruit in the adult. While one's whole life is certainly not determined by one's temperament, temperament does determine how we do things—whether we do them slowly and deliberately or in a last-minute frenzy; whether we rigidly stick to our prejudices or are open to changing our minds; whether we like solitude or groups, loud music or quiet; whether we're "naturally" sunny or dour.

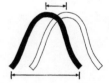

In the beginning, all of us differ in fundamental ways, such as in our characteristic emotion, degree of shyness, and level of activity. From very early on, there is something constant about the way we act and react amid all the tumult, change, and growth of life. The next chapters, then, look into these dimensions of temperament.

Chapter 5

Three Dimensions of Temperament

Identical twin men, now age thirty, were separated at birth and raised in different countries by their respective adoptive parents. Both kept their lives neat—neat to the point of pathology. Their clothes were preened, appointments met precisely on time, hands scrubbed regularly to a raw, red color. When the first was asked why he felt the need to be so clean, his answer was plain.

"My mother. When I was growing up she always kept the house perfectly ordered. She insisted on every little thing returned to its proper place, the clocks—we had dozens of clocks—each set to the same noonday chime. She insisted on this, you see. I learned from her. What else could I do?"

The man's identical twin, just as much a perfectionist with soap and water, explained his own behavior this way: "The reason is quite simple. I'm reacting to my mother, who was an absolute slob."

PETER AND ALEXANDER NEUBAUER, *NATURE'S THUMBPRINT*

Why do I need everything completely shipshape? Why am I always getting into battles with my boss and my children? Why is my sister so restless while I'm quite happy to sit home and read? What's wrong with me, or is there something wrong with her? Why am I always so happy while my wife is often sad, even when we're both on vacation? My brother is a much harder worker than I am; how can I match him? Most of us ask ourselves these questions at least occasionally; others concentrate on them almost constantly and spend lots of time and money to come up with answers.

There is considerable evidence that much of our basic temperament is *inherent* to us, whether it is directly inherited or not.[1] However, we don't take much notice of these inherent differences in practice. School exams, for example, may be set up in a way that suits one individual's temperament better than another's, but everyone has to take them in the same way. There are easy ways of determining temperament (through administering certain paper-and-pencil tests and through measuring a person's salivary and cardiac reactions when he or she tastes lemon juice, as mentioned in the last chapter), but one doesn't often hear of a therapist or a teacher applying such information to his or her work. People with differing temperaments have different requirements for sedatives, yet I know of no anesthetist who takes these kinds of differences into account before putting a patient out during surgery.

Why are these differences ignored? Some fear that any sort of biological determinism, like that of Galton, will be used as an excuse for all sorts of discrimination, oppression, or worse. What's more, while teachers, parents, and developmental psychologists acknowledge that children show quite distinct temperaments from an early age, their scientific interest lies in exploring how "children in general" progress, learn, and develop. In schools, the *average* is what counts, not the countless differences. It's a practical matter, too, since the greatest good for the greatest number is often the cheapest to achieve.

Psychologists, to consider one important group, need to reconsider seriously their approach to understanding mind and behavior, as the dominion of this once-popular science is disappearing before its practitioners' very eyes. At one time, we could find works on human nature by many diverse authors, from behaviorist B. F. Skinner, to psychiatrists Sigmund Freud and Eric Erikson, to psychobiologist Donald Hebb. Now, however, psychology's scope has been limited at one end by cognitive science and neuroscience, which have taken charge of much of the analysis of the mind, and by the death of behaviorism at the other, which has eliminated much of the practical analysis of behavior.

---

1. I am using the word *inherent* because it specifies that a quality is a fundamental part of the person, whether we can follow the exact lines of inheritance or not.

Where important works were once readily available and widely discussed, serious psychology is getting replaced in most bookstores with self-help and "recovery" books that stress how we're all victims of our family. What is left in the domain of scientific psychology may well be the understanding of individuality: why some people can't remember faces, while others can't recall places; why some are always on the go, can't sit still, and relax by racing bobsleds, while others like serious couch time; why some put a positive "spin" on everything, while others dump on and dampen down all that reaches them. There might be, too, a chance to consider how our individuality may lead to disorders. This chance would be greatly improved if psychiatrists knew more of psychology and vice versa.

Parents know better, and know that their children are born with very definite dispositions. "He was always a quiet little boy," they'll say, or "She was always climbing trees and looking for excitement."

The same may be true with regards to how active we may be, how excitable, how emotional, all of which are measurable differences at birth. Our singularity isn't completely fixed on day one of birth or day one of conception, but we all have an inherent temperament—to be sociable and outgoing or shy and withdrawn.

There has always been a belief that external physical characteristics and individuality are related, a belief so popular in the 1700s that people selected wet nurses because of it. Women who had dark complexion and dark hair were chosen because they would be easy-going and easy to manage. Many in Northern Europe were happy to believe that characteristics such as blond hair, lean build, and light skin would predict behavior, that the dark-haired, stockier, Latinate person must have an innate disposition for "hot blood," while the stolid, slender, suicidal Swede would get some of his taciturnity from his genes.

After Darwin wrote *Origin of Species*, it became reasonable to believe that groups of people who lived in different areas of the world, like birds separated from other birds for millennia, would develop different physical characteristics to adapt to the situation. Some of the era also thought that different body types would produce different susceptibilities to disease, that brown-eyed people would have gall bladder problems while blue-eyed adults would have anemia.

As we discussed in Chapter One, categorizing people is an intuitively appealing idea, and theories of types and temperaments can be found throughout history. Often, these categories have been based on presumed differences in biology. The Greeks classified people according to their predominant "humors" (fluids in the body). Depressed (melancholic-type) people were thought to have too much black bile, while too much yellow bile resulted in an excitable (choleric-type) person. An excess of blood accounted for emotional expressiveness (sanguine type), and too much phlegm (phlegmatic type) was thought to result in a person who was unflappable.

Modern psychologists use the word *temperament* to refer to a person's predisposition to respond to specific events in a specific way; thus, temperament refers to the style rather than to the content of behavior. We might say, as do Thomas and Chess, that temperament is the "how" of behavior, not the what.

Personality, on the other hand, is the full-blown complex of reactions that distinguish an individual. We would need to list hundreds of particulars in order to describe a person we know well: slow to anger; tough when provoked; generally calm; likes travel, Mozart, Madonna; reads the sports pages; is generous; finds it tough to commit to someone; athletic. But not all of these characteristics are intrinsic to a person, and too many factors enter in to make any real analysis of the "fully flowered" individual possible, no matter the many books and programs available. Trying to predict how anyone will act in all complexity is a bit like trying to predict the weather in some random month from now in a random place at a random time.

Temperament, on the other hand, is more general,

Each of us receives different amounts of humors

more basic than is the whole complex personality; it concerns whether one does everything slowly or quickly, whether one seeks excitement or sits alone, whether one is highly expressive or inhibited, joyous or sullen. Temperament is the basic rootstock of individuality, our basic shape, which is ready to be molded into different characteristics by other forces. One can be a musician who plays slowly or quickly, with small hand movements or sweeping ones; one can be aggressive in the stock market with a quiet temperament or a boisterous one; one can be a dutiful mother whether one is excitable or calm.

Predispositions in temperament are some of the main roots of adult abilities. A placid baby most often develops into an easygoing teenager. As we've already seen, shy children differ from outgoing children in their limbic systems, which influence lifelong differences in inhibition and arousal.

Each of us has implicit theories of individuality. We use them not only to type other people ("Joe is an honest person") but to predict ("Morgan is generous, so I'll ask her if I can borrow a ten"). Belief in the importance of traits and types rests on the assumption that knowing a person's characteristics will tell us something about how that person will behave.

Such systems of types usually provide a way of describing an individual in absolute terms: introverted or extroverted, stable or neurotic. A type is a cluster of related traits—a superfactor. Like character traits, types offer a description of personality that implies predictability. The Greek classification scheme just described is one system of typology, while the American Psychiatric Association's *Diagnostic and Statistical Manual of Mental Disorders* offers a way to type disorders.

The psychiatrist William Sheldon advanced a theory of personality based on body type. He classified three basic types of human individuals: ectomorphs are lean, delicate people who are quiet and nonassertive; endomorphs are buxom and peaceful; and mesomorphs are muscular and combative. Further, Sheldon measured the proportions of hundreds of boys whom he categorized as juvenile delinquents and concluded that they were generally mesomorphs.

It is quite possible that given a particular build, a person will act like the related stereotype because this is what is expected.

So an ectomorph may become more of a quiet intellectual type, the endomorph a kind of relaxed sociable homebody, and the mesomorph more athletic because of social conditioning as much as heredity.

We tend to see how a person behaves and then attribute that behavior to a basic personality trait. Most of us assume that these traits consistently influence others' behavior. We think that someone who is honest never lies to friends, does not cheat, and doesn't steal. But we are so often wrong. Some psychologists question whether people really are consistent enough across situations to make knowledge of traits useful in predicting behavior. This very complexity, however, is probably what keeps most of us interested in each other, as we puzzle over how to piece together an accurate picture of another person.

The three basic dimensions of individuality that I review in the following chapters are aspects of temperament. I make no claim that these are the only three, but these three, as said earlier, combine three sources. The first source is the evidence of large brain systems that control movements and organize sequences of actions. The second is the evidence from the countless millions of psychological tests, and the third is from clinical observation. Each individual has a "set point," like that of a thermostat, for each of these three basic dimensions. Where one is "set" on each of these dimensions seems to endure within the individual, and these settings can tell us a great deal. Understanding that someone is a person who needs a lot of new stimulation, for example, might lead us to expect this person to be outgoing, excitable, and quick to establish intimacy. However, we might want to know that this intimacy may not last as long as it would with other people.

The basics of individuality are laid down early: whether we're quick or slow, easily angered or not, sunny or sullen, active or idle. The high-level parts of the brain develop diversely in different individuals, depending on experiences and a myriad of factors. Simply put, three primitive systems that evolved long before human beings ever were a glimmer in God's eye are the primitive main roots of individuality. Each person lies at a point on the dimension of the system. To recap:

The first of these systems has the task of alerting the cortex, sending a stream of arousal messages to the higher parts of the brain. Many of these messages travel through the limbic system in the midbrain, where emotions are controlled. The limbic system sends out its own stream of messages to "wake up" the person to an event, such as "large object approaching fast!"

The second system involves the interplay between the ancient lower brain centers, which have precise preprogrammed plans for action, and the more recently evolved higher brain centers, which try to regulate these spontaneous actions and make plans of their own.

The third system governs the overall feeling tone of the person—whether one is sweet or sour, warm or cold; whether one characteristically approaches the world or withdraws from it.

Let us look more closely now at each of these systems and at how they control the three basic dimensions of temperament. We'll begin with gain, then go on to deliberation-liberation and feelings.

Chapter 6

High and Low Amplification
Setting the Gain Control

Let's go back, way back, to the beginning of the brain. The brain has its own archaeology. Just as there are layers to an archaeological dig, there are "layers" to the brain—different levels of functions that have developed as the brain evolved. The structures seem to be laid on top of each other, and these separate parts of the brain have, loosely speaking, minds of their own. There are processes for maintaining alertness, for feeling emotions, for sensing danger, for comparing sensory information, for avoiding scarcity, and for many other functions.

The human brain's ancient systems provide the roots of our individuality. Many scientists think that the brain's structure and functioning evolved atop the neural mechanisms of our immediate ancestors, the primates, which developed from earlier mammals and, before that, from more primitive vertebrates. In turn, these vertebrates inherited many of their neural circuits and routines from earlier and simpler multicellular creatures.

The brain stem, the oldest part of the brain, evolved over 500 million years ago, before the evolution of mammals. The brain stem runs basic life support. In the center of the brain stem and traveling its full length is a core of neural tissue known as the reticular activating system (RAS). Like a bell, the RAS alerts the cortex to arriving information, such as "visual stimulus on its way." When a sleeping dog is stimulated by electrodes in the RAS, it awakens immediately and searches the environment. The RAS also controls the general level of arousal—wakefulness, sleep, attention, excitement, and so on. An exciting or worrying thought, a loud noise, or an alarming sight will trigger the RAS.

Most sensory information from the outside world enters the lower brain stem. The brain stem's thalamus then classifies this information ("Is it visual or auditory?") and relays it to the appropriate part of the cortex.

It is in the thalamus of the brain stem that the incoming information is amplified or reduced as it passes through, much as an audio signal passes through the amplification or the "gain" control on an audio amplifier. The impulses travel in both directions: arousing or exciting messages are sent upward to the cortex, where thought and memory and images occur, and inhibitory impulses come back down from the cortex to the brain stem to reduce the amount of activity in the input systems.

The average setting for the input system in the brain stem differs for each of us, and the amount of amplification influences everything we do. Some, with low amplification in their nervous system, are starved for stimulation all the time; others, with very high amplification, are surfeited. The rest of us are somewhere in the middle.

Have you ever gone into a disco, with lights flashing, people dancing and gyrating, and music blaring? Or entered a church so quiet you could hear a pin drop? Or watched the stars on a clear night? For some people, whom I'll call the "high gainers," the world is very loud indeed; for others, the "low gainers," it is subdued. Some people respond to this low level of input by becoming very active and needing a lot of stimulation, while the high gainers often become very quiet, seeking little.

Deirdre and Harry have been married for twenty-five years. Even though they are truly fond of each other, both would agree that their marriage has been an irritable one; they have somehow gotten along, but their personal styles are very different. Before marriage, Deirdre had dreams of being an actress. She is a demonstrative and friendly person; she laughs a lot and always attempts to be the life and soul of every party. She is unremittingly interested in people, events, and everything theatrical.

Shyness is unknown to her. She'll approach anybody about anything and is always prepared to have a conversation on any subject, or at least to "have a go," unconcerned about whether she knows anything about it or not. Her doctor husband used to wince at her willingness to entertain everybody all the time; she seldom let him get a word in edgewise. Not that he would want to—he is so overwhelmed in social groups that nobody is aware how much he knows or how interesting he can be. His wife thought he presented himself as a "dry old stick-in-the-mud"; he thought her social ease was "vulgar" and "embarrassing."

By compromising, however, which mostly meant that Deirdre toned down her personality, they managed to get along— and might have done so forever, had not Deirdre contracted a dramatic and intense illness. She was rushed to the hospital, where everyone made such a fuss of her that the extrovert actress she had more or less kept under wraps for years emerged triumphant. She was queen of the hospital ward. The nurses adored her. The other patients thought she was wonderful. So great was the discomfort of her introverted husband under these circumstances that it was sometimes hard to know whether her illness or the reemergence of her nature upset him more.

The difference between being outgoing and impulsive and being withdrawn and shy is central to individuality. No individual is exclusively one or the other. Just as human beings range from being very short to very tall, with most of us somewhere in

High-gain people turn down the
outside world, low gainers
turn it up

the middle, so are we all "set" somewhere between extreme high and extreme low gain.

On first consideration of this information, you might assume that the person with a brain highly tuned for arousal would be forever looking for action and excitement. But it doesn't work that way: the quiet types are naturally *more aroused* than the gregarious ones. This is why introverts tend to go for the quiet life because they *already have enough going on inside without having to seek excitement.*

There's the paradox; those "high gainers" who are highly aroused internally are not the people who are racing around the world, seeking new excitement. They are the ones curled up on a sofa reading quietly. They don't seek many friends. They don't like loud music; they don't even prefer crunchy peanut butter to smooth. They don't often want to make much noise or move around as much, so their activity is more tranquil.

By contrast, the outgoing, party-animal types who are intensely interested in loud music, who love going out often and to all hours, who enjoy fast driving or parachute jumping, who are often tangled up in complex business or personal dramas, are the ones who have a low-gain nervous system. They need all this excitement and stimulation to keep going. The "low gainers"—whose inner worlds are quiet—need to seek or produce the noise themselves. Thus, many of them have more trouble with the law than do introverts, and they have more business and marital conflicts, do more risky things, and make and lose numerous friends; they're often divorcing, changing jobs, running rapids, and so on.

Those highly extroverted report better sex lives: they have more partners, they do it more often, and they feel less guilty about it. They also do better on exams and in primary school, while introverts seem to do better at university. Introverts usually do better at tasks that require careful attention, while extroverts usually make hopeless radar officers, for example, as their attention quickly wanders from the screen.

Introvert/Extrovert Differences

There are many physiological studies that illuminate these differences. The brain's blood flow is related to the arousal of the cortex. In one study, a group of people filled in a questionnaire designed to indicate whether they were low or high gainers. The experimenter then measured the blood flow in parts of their brain and found that the high gainers had a higher rate than the low gainers.

High gainers do seem to experience the world differently from low gainers; the world is "loud" to high gainers, so they turn the volume down, as it were. One study showed how this works in the brain. When a sudden sound or light appears, we have a characteristic cortex reaction, called the "evoked response." In this study, groups of extroverts and introverts[1] were exposed to increasingly intense visual and auditory stimuli while the evoked responses of their brain wave patterns were recorded. Once the stimulus, either the light or noise, reached a high level, the introverts tended to decrease the intensity of the stimulus that the brain received from the outside (this is known as reduction). Extroverts, on the other hand, turned their stimuli up (a process called augmentation).

If you give a high- and a low-gain person the same dose of a sedative, what happens? Low gainers fall asleep with a low dose, and high gainers require a higher dosage for sedation than do low gainers. Extroverts, being low gain, are less aroused than introverts. Being chronically aroused, introverts are also more sensitive to stimuli at all levels.

Introverts are also more sensitive to barely detectable stimuli and have lower pain thresholds than do extroverts. These two groups have the same

Low-gain craves a quiet world

---

1. Low gainer and "extrovert," high gainer and "introvert" are strongly related but are not completely synonymous. While extroverts are low gain and introverts high gain, one could also have a low-gain person who isn't an extrovert—one who satisfies her or his craving for stimulation through massages and listening to loud music at home, for instance, rather than through socializing and the like.

reactions to the "lemon-drop test" as do shy and sociable young children. Put four drops of lemon juice on an adult extrovert's tongue for twenty seconds, and he or she will salivate little, but extreme introverts will show an increase of about one gram of saliva. The high gainers mobilize their internal system, producing saliva or, as did the children studied in Chapter Four, increasing heart rate. The similarity of these findings would lead me to guess that the "shy" and "inhibited" young children we discussed are similar in temperament to the adults we class as introverted. However, the same studies haven't been done on both groups.

The reaction to external stimuli may well explain why extroverts do better under pressure, since the high level of stimulation that such pressure provides—and that would tip an introvert over the edge—is just what extroverts need to perform at their best. Extroverts have naturally low levels of arousal, so they seek stimulation outside, hence their high interest in parties, sex, and dangerous sports.

What is happening in the brain stem is that the RAS is tuned differently in low gainers and high gainers. Given standard conditions of external stimulation, introverts' RAS is set higher, making them more highly aroused. Since everyone seeks an optimal level of excitement in daily life, introverts, being more aroused to begin with, need less stimulation than extroverts. An introvert's cortex, then, inhibits the lower brain centers more than an extrovert's does.

Extroverts have a better short-term memory but also forget things more quickly, while introverts remember things for a longer period of time but have difficulty remembering things under stress—such as during exams. Extroverts are more rebellious because they form conditioned reflexes less easily; thus, they are more difficult to train. Extroverts also talk more and make more eye contact.

Extroverts feel good more often during the day than do introverts. Two psychologists administered an extroversion scale from the Eysenck inventory to college undergraduates, who also completed mood reports daily for six to eight weeks. Each night before they went to bed, these people filled out a form that asked them to rate their current mood on different adjective scales, such as happy, joyful, or pleased; unhappy, depressed, frustrated, worried, anxious, angry, or hostile. More positive responses were strongly associated with extroversion.

Why do extroverts feel more positive than introverts? One reason is that extroverts may be less responsive to punishment than introverts. Introverts appear to dwell on the negative features of social situations; they recall less positive information about themselves and rate others less positively in social situations, and they are much more sensitive to punishment and negativity. Extroverts are much more likely to continue acting in the face of punishment and frustration.

Consider President Clinton in the presidential campaign of 1992. He faced an amazing amount of negativity about his draft record, marital infidelity, veracity, and the like. However, he soldiered on and learned how to deal with it. But not all extroverts are as studious as is Mr. Clinton. Because most of them respond so little to punishment, they often learn less in complex situations. They typically fail to pause following punishment to learn from their mistakes; instead, they push ahead to the next challenge.

This also happens in other situations. Extroverts expend considerable effort to listen to loud jazz music and look at bright lights, creating their own disco effect, while introverts work hard to avoid these. Extroverts choose higher levels of noise in a learning situation and perform better in the presence of noise, while introverts perform better in quiet.

One extreme form of low gain is sensation seeking. Sensation seekers want more of everything; they seek a larger variety in sexual activities and a larger number of sexual partners for both heterosexual and homosexual adults, males and females. They tend to use recreational drugs, such as marijuana and amphetamines. They smoke more cigarettes, and they fancy more intense taste experiences; consequently, they prefer spicy, sour, and crunchy foods. They engage more often in physically risky activities, such as parachuting, motorcycling, scuba diving, and fire fighting.

They volunteer, but for unusual types of experiments such as sensory deprivation, hypnosis, and drug studies, and also for unusual types of activities such as encounter groups, alpha training, and transcendental meditation. They begin conversations, they speak more than high gainers do, and they tend to be selected by others as leaders of the group. They tend to score high on measures of dominance. Not surprisingly, they prefer complex artistic forms to simple ones, since these give more stimulation, but they also prefer the color blue. They are likely to be impulsive. Among heterosexual couples, they tend to be romantically attracted to and to marry people who are also sensation seekers.

The English Dimensional Approach

*I*mportant recent investigators of this dimension include Hans Eysenck and Gordon Claridge in England. Eysenck came from Germany to England in about 1934 to escape the Nazis. He employed hundreds of people in analyzing thousands of questionnaire items and determined that one major dimension in which persons differ is extroversion-introversion, a derivation of gain.

Eysenck wasn't the first to identify these dimensions. Galen in the second century A.D. identified this dimension, as well as Immanuel Kant and Carl Jung. One of the earliest attempts was the medieval idea of the four humors, which described people as being either melancholic, sanguine, choleric, or phlegmatic. People who are extroverted are outgoing, impulsive, uninhibited, have many contacts and frequently take part in group activities. Introverts are quiet, retiring, introspective, and not socially active.

If you are an introvert or an extrovert, are you forever the same? Can you change? For most people, introversion and extroversion are remarkably stable. Outgoing children, who are less aroused, tend to stay that way, as do timid ones. Aaron Connolly analyzed data from a fifty-year longitudinal study where subjects had rated themselves in 1935–1938, 1954–1955, and 1980–1981 and found that the consistency of how they rated themselves as extroverts was very strong.

Inherited Tendencies

*T*here is good evidence that this responsivity to the external world is inherited. For example, extrovert identical twins are more alike than fraternal twins in how sociable they are. What is more, identical twins are much more likely to be similar than are other siblings in whether they augment or reduce stimuli and whether they are easy or difficult to knock out with drugs. Some studies even find different innate brain wave patterns associated with extroverts and introverts, and these seem to be inherited.

But what you are given biologically can be shaped by what happens to you; temperament doesn't lock you into a particular personality just because it is inherited. In the case of this dimension, sociability is likely to be encouraged by teachers and parents while impulsivity is likely to be discouraged, but you would expect the discouragement to be less consistent and effective.

Something primitive and basic like the amount our nervous system turns up or down the world has, then, very general and far-reaching effects. A person may crave stimulation throughout her or his whole life, seeking danger in sports, relationships, and work in order to be aroused. This tendency doesn't govern *what* anyone will do—whether he or she becomes a broker or a dancer (but an extrovert would be very dangerous as an air traffic controller, since they would fall asleep with the boredom!)—but how they do it.

I'll say more on this later, but it's important to realize that this dimension is intrinsic, and it determines the amount of bustle and stimulation we need. It means that couples who don't have the same level of gain, for instance, had best take note of these differences and accept them, knowing that they don't indicate anything "personal." Just as we need to accept our different requirements for salt on our food, so we need to accept our differences in the need for stimulation of all sorts.

Chapter 7

Deliberation-Liberation

Organizing Actions and Thoughts

Early in May 1990, George Harrison, former Beatle, received a series of death threats in the mail. Within days, British police were questioning an "aging hippie" whose compulsion for detail was so great that he had not only sent the threatening letters but he had also put his address (in Battersea, South London) on them, according to the London *Daily Telegraph* and *Daily Mail*.

The second continuum concerns how much an individual deliberates about, and thus regulates, his or her actions or how open he or she is to the spontaneous experiences of the moment. Of course, everyone has to do both to live, as even opening a can requires organization, and responding to changes in traffic or to people crossing the street demands a spontaneous update of whatever plan one has in mind. Nevertheless, different individuals are set at different points on a scale of how well and how often and in what detail they deliberate about and then control their daily actions. Here are two examples.

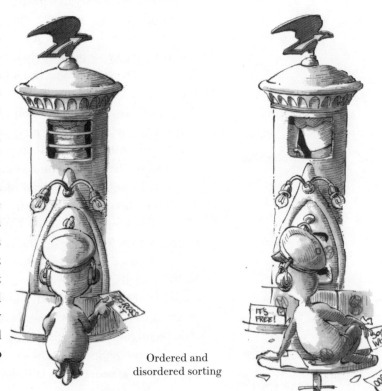

Ordered and disordered sorting

Meriel lives in Scotland, and her life, described from the outside, is quite unrestrained, although she would not see it that way. She has a good education and is well above average intelligence, but the impetuousness that has dominated her life has meant that neither she nor her children have a secure base.

Her children are from different husbands and range in age from twenty-two to two. Currently she works as a fortune-teller in a fairground. She takes off from time to time with new men or strikes out on new "trips" or new career ideas; she sends her children to stay with different members of the family, and at the first sign of trouble takes them back and sends them somewhere else.

Her reputation among people who know her is of being untrustworthy at worst, misguided at best. She has a good heart—but is wholly at the mercy of her whims. She never sees the whole story, only small episodes at a time. As with the impulses in an electronic signal, she starts off on a new enthusiasm with a rush of energy that dies away after a fairly short time; then there is a gap (to sort out the latest mess) before the next impulse. The next inspiration always arrives. She might even kill herself—on an impulse.

Compare her with Aurelus, who rises around 5:00 every morning to write his novels before going to his job as an editor. He works the same hour and a half, from 5:45 to 7:15, on his writing each morning. At 7:15, he gets dressed for his office work.

And how he gets dressed is certainly relevant. His closet always contains five sets of neatly pressed clothes. They're not just good clothes; they are well thought out outfits, ordered and organized as to the day of the week. There's an Armani, a Valentino, a brown jacket with a pair of black slacks, an outfit with a blazer. Each has its own specific shirt, tie, and the relevant accessories. If it's Monday, this must be Valentino. He has a second complete set of clothes for going on the road.

When he buys something new, it replaces one of the "weekly office" outfits, and one of these moves down to a spot on the road team. When he's done with the road-show clothes? He gives them to a relative. What a system, but it works for him. Might not be so wonderful for Meriel, this prodigal deliberation about what to wear.

Keeping lists of kitchen objects to be cleaned regularly, codifying precise procedures through the law, separating feelings from rational judgment when buying a house—all speak to the virtues of deliberate and conscious decisions on action. At the other end, relaxed spontaneity is liberating; it underlies restful moments and low stress, as well as letting the intuitive—some might say unconscious—brain processes come forward. Vacations are a way in which we move ourselves up or down on this continuum. Many modern workers, who have highly regulated lives, seek vacations in an unstructured, carefree environment that liberates them from planning. Very few people want to take a vacation by doing tax returns or spell-checking on a word processor.

I've chosen "deliberation-liberation" as the description of this continuum in part because it's accurate and in part because it sounds good. Deliberation involves regulation of activity, planning, usually a sequence of distinct and separated actions: "First we'll reserve for the twenty-third to the twenty-seventh at campsite number 201, then we'll go to the camping store, then we'll buy some tent poles and check them for size, then we'll get a tent that fits our car, then we'll get a road map and plan the best route. . . ." I use "liberation" to mean spontaneous activity, openness to new experiences, and no boundaries between actions or thoughts and feelings, all happening more at once, in the "flow": "Let's go to the mountains now."

We can all easily recognize where someone sits on the continuum of deliberation-liberation. At the center but slightly toward the liberated side are what we call free spirits, and on the other side of center are the careful sort who plan out each week and every vacation in detail. Further from free-spirithood might be those who are creative in all spheres, who feel free to follow uncharted lines of association and have an "artistic temperament," and on the other side would be those with a rigid accountancy or legal mentality, who work everything out sequentially, logically, in order, where all is checked and balanced. As we move further away, impulsivity and compulsivity would appear on

OCD COMPULSIVE ARMY ORGANIZED NORMAL INTERESTING SLOB CREATIVE FLAKEY SCHIZOPHRENIC each side, and furthest away would be schizotypal thought and schizophrenia itself on one side and obsessive-compulsive disorder on the other.

Most of us, for most of our lives, mix deliberated planning and openness to the moment, although we all have our set point on this continuum for different activities. In each case, the layers between us and the world are thicker or thinner, more bounded or more open.

The Frontal Lobes and Limbic System

This system seems to vary depending not on the reticular activating system of the brain but on the relationship between the control centers in the frontal cortex and the lower brain centers. In the organization of the brain, the frontal lobes handle conscious decisions, while the lower centers provide the impulses for spontaneous actions. Before there was a "civilized" world, before there was language, before there were morning commutes, animals evolved a set of spontaneous, automatic reactions that would get them through the day. Loud noise—run; specific animal in view—attack or hide; dehydrated—drink something. These lower brain processes operate on their own, spontaneously, without conscious control from the top parts of the human brain, yet they control our most basic survival reactions, like keeping our blood at the right temperature and sending hormones all over the body.

Deliberation-liberation is strongly influenced by the human frontal lobe–limbic system circuits. The frontal lobes lie at the intersection of the neural pathways in the cortex, brain stem, and limbic system that transport information about people and events in the world and informa-

RANDOM CREATIVE THOUGHT FROM CORTEX

INFORMATION ABOUT PEOPLE AND THE WORLD

EMOTIONS FROM LIMBIC SYSTEM

thalamatic

HYPOTHALAMUS (LIMBIC SYSTEM)

LIMBIC THRESHOLD SET POINT AT WHICH EMOTIONS ARE TRIGGERED

tion from the limbic system about the body's own state. The frontal lobes also control the impulses from the limbic area.

While it is not possible to find a specific location for the self in the brain, the functions related to what we call the self seem to depend on decisions made in the frontal lobes. Different forms of emotions are represented within each of the frontal lobes, as well as some control of the expression of emotions. The self-system in the frontal lobes influences us to seek out different information, to remember differently, and to think and evaluate differently. In tragic cases, damage to the frontal lobes results in the inability to know on a long-term basis who one is.

The degree to which one plans one's life may well relate to deliberation about their actions. The frontal lobes participate in planning, decision making, and purposeful behavior. If they are destroyed or removed, the individual becomes incapable of planning, carrying out, or comprehending a complex action or idea and is unable to adapt to new situations. Such a person simply can't decide which of the possible alternatives he or she should choose. These people are unable to focus their attention, and they

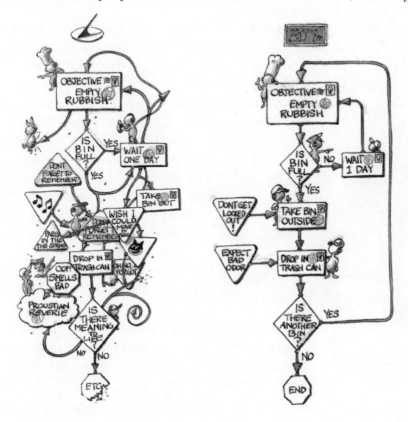

Deliberated and liberated
schemes for taking
out the trash

become distracted by irrelevant stimuli. Their language and consciousness are fine, but the loss of the ability to adapt and plan ahead makes those other abilities useless.

Two neurosurgical patients with frontal lobe damage, studied by the French neurologist Lhermitte, illustrate how the regulatory functions need intact frontal lobes. One patient named Marie, who had a tumor removed from the frontal cortex, sat with her neurologist in his office. Seeing medical instruments on the desk, she immediately assumed a line of action: she began to take the physician's blood pressure, then used the tongue depressor to look into his throat, and then banged his knee with the hammer. She pronounced him in good health. When she came into a buffet in a lecture room, she unstacked a set of chairs, put out the glasses, and offered drinks all around. She was acting in a good sequence, a sequence appropriate for the hostess of a party, but it wasn't her party. The mechanism whereby we deliberate about the appropriateness of our actions had gone awry. Another time, Marie, seeing a hypodermic needle, took it from the table and asked Lhermitte to pull down his pants in preparation for a shot. Unfortunately, Dr. Lhermitte stops the story there.

Pierre, also a patient with frontal lobe damage, got upset when he was put in front of a cosmetic table. He found a gun in the room and excitedly began to load it in front of his physician. This time Lhermitte does tell us that the experiment was terminated. In the same situation, Marie picked up the cosmetics and began to make herself up, then saw knitting needles and started to use them, then saw a broom and began to sweep.

When Pierre was at a party in a room with paintings, his doctor uttered the word *museum*. Pierre began to prance about, looking carefully at the composition of each painting, posing in the way art buyers do and making pseudocritical remarks.

These people knew how to do things, such as how to act the way art buyers do in a gallery, but they were no longer capable of deliberately deciding to do these things—they just did them.

Internal sorting

The overall planning function had been destroyed, but pieces of similar plans remained, ready to be activated by impulse.

People differ on how much the emotional brain centers impinge on their day-to-day lives and how easily they keep different parts of their lives apart. For highly controlled, often highly verbal people, "everything in its place" comes naturally, while a more diffuse style is the norm for others, even when it's not wanted.

The more diffuse style is also associated with how intense and changeable someone's emotional responses are. Such "liberated" people often overrespond and find it difficult to return to a normal state; they often complain of vague physical problems.

To go back to the garden metaphor, one person's brain might be like a professionally run farm with every crop set in order, while another is more like an open field, with everything free and merging together.

Hartmann and the Concept of Boundaries

*P*sychiatrist Ernest Hartmann, in *Boundaries in the Mind,* makes a distinction similar to the one I'm proposing; he distinguishes between people with thin and thick boundaries. One patient of his always impressed him with his precision and organization. When they would talk, the patient would sometimes open his attaché case, which was divided into separate compartments precisely fitted for pens, pads, files, calculators, and so on. "There was never a loose pencil, or scrap of paper, never a speck of dust. He would immediately lay his hands on the paper he wanted, read it or show it to me, file it back in its place and snap the case shut. It seemed to me that his mind is much like his attaché case, or rather that he had organized his attaché case the way his mind was organized."

The analysis of boundaries shows that some people focus sharply and cleanly on one thing in the environment or in their lives. They can deal with it and go on to the next thing. Other people are fuzzier. They seem to be able to deal with things all at once; they are, if you like, broadly based rather than narrowly based. One liberated person who was tested said, "This is too much coming in at once; I can never focus on just one thing at a time."

Looking at a picture, one deliberate soul might say, "I see a brown house on a green meadow." A more liberated person would say, "The light in this picture is so thick I can almost taste it," or "That paint on the shutters is so shrill I can hear the tone in it." For the liberated person, perceptions are not strongly separated.

Similarly, states of awareness and states of sleep may merge in liberators, while they are separate in deliberators. Highly deliberate people often ignore their dreams, while a more liberated person may find the difference between dreaming and waking difficult to notice. They may be deeply affected by their dreams all the time. They are also more able to have lucid dreams, those in which one is conscious of dreaming.

People's occupations seem to differ depending on each person's place on the deliberation-liberation continuum. In Hartmann's study of forty people, the twenty deliberators broke down as follows: six were women and fourteen were men, all of them were married, and their average age was fifty-one. Their occupations were largely in business, law, and engineering. There were three homemakers, one architect, one electrician, and one technician.

They reported very few nightmares and very few dreams of any sort. They were fairly "normal" and fairly conventional. None of them seemed to have any psychiatric-type problems, although they described themselves as "unfeeling," "rigid," "obsessive." When they did dream, Hartmann reports that they often dreamed about being boxed in.

> I was in a room, squarish in shape, with concrete walls on three sides. The fourth side was all glass or unglazed and open. The view seemed to be from inside the bottom of a large concrete dam looking out at the spillway some [undetermined] feet below. There were three of us in the room; two were college friends. We were joined by a fourth person, whose name I don't recall, who came toward us from what seemed like a long, small, square concrete tunnel.
>
> ERNEST HARTMANN, *BOUNDARIES OF THE MIND*

The twenty liberated people in this study were very different: seventeen women and three men; of the nineteen for whom information was obtained, twelve were single, six were married, and one was divorced; four were homemakers, three were teachers, two were artists, and of the rest one was a laborer, one a nurse, one a counselor. No lawyers, no engineers, no business executives.

These people remembered dreams almost every night. And their dreams influenced their waking life to a great extent. In these people and in other "liberators" who have been studied, their openness was felt as a kind of skinlessness.

> My father skinned me with a knife just the way one skins a rabbit. He skinned me and my sisters, and threw us in a heap. I was lying there with no skin, quivering, bloody; it was horribly painful, I could feel everything.

ERNEST HARTMANN, *BOUNDARIES OF THE MIND*

The degree of "skinlessness"—when one's thought is so liberated from one's plans that events in the external world come right in—can, if mild, enhance creativity; if strong, it can affect a person's sanity. Indeed, such people, when they are in need of help, are often described as "sensitive," "fragile," and "schizotypal." The great psychiatrist Manfred Bleuler thought that the difference between the normal and the schizophrenic was that the schizophrenic loosens control over associated thought. We'll discuss further the relationship between the normal and the disordered in Chapter Nine.

Indicators of those at the less-bordered end of the scale on this dimension are whether one sometimes experiences great fluctuations in mood, becoming sometimes happy and sometimes depressed without any apparent reason, and whether one's mind wanders while trying to concentrate. These people get "lost in thought," "spaced out," even when taking part in a conversation; their feelings are easily hurt; they're irritable and changeable. This changeability can dominate their lives, as it may make their emotional relationships, as well as their careers, difficult. Because they're often interrupting themselves, they often have difficulty getting somewhere on time, to the inconvenience of their friends. A number of such people of my acquaintance have, independently, been given the nickname, "The late Mr. (Ms. or Mrs.)," indicating the edgy hostility that they sometimes inspire in others in their lives.

In psychotherapy, a highly deliberated client may find it difficult to free-associate and to tell someone what's on his or her mind, while a liberated one may find it very easy to free-associate.

A deliberator may get a quick start in the morning. One man says, "I just snap awake. It's like something clicks, and I'm wide awake." In contrast, those at the liberated end have much more trouble "getting themselves together," since their actions and ideas are more changeable and fluid. A much more open person may say, "It often takes me half an hour or an hour to make sure I'm really awake in the morning, especially when I've just had a vivid dream." Where the danger for the highly organized is that their ability to snap into place may also snap an inappropriate re-action into action, the danger for the more loosely organized is that they will act, like Meriel, on one impulse after another.

One of Dr. Hartmann's clients, Heather, is liberated on our con-tinuum.[1] She is twenty-eight, unmarried, and lives alone; she has had tempestuous relationships with men; she works as a music teacher. She came to see Hartmann initially because of nightmares and anxiety, but she also needed to examine and organize her life. She remembers herself as being extremely sensitive, so that things that might have had less effect on others would hurt her. She says, "Since I couldn't keep things out, everything got to me all the time."

When she found a rabbit injured by a passing car, she was in-consolable and could not keep the picture of the suffering rabbit out of her mind for a long time. Her brothers would take advan-tage of her by talking about killing animals just to get her an-noyed. She became a vegetarian because she could not bear the idea of anyone killing an animal so that others could eat it. Heather had a stormy life with passionate friendships and love affairs often ending in rejection. She's a good example of the prob-lems presented by being extremely open.

Such people often have intense but short-lived relationships. They may fall madly in love and live only for that relationship, but then something may occur that leads the person to terminate the relationship.

An education that involves systematic organization and planning, like law school, tends to be good for highly regulated people. This may be one reason why it's commonly—and not per-

---

1. Dr. Hartmann, of course, doesn't use the terms *liberation* and *deliberation,* but I am extending the concept of this continuum to encompass his interesting discussion of people with thin and thick boundaries.

haps incorrectly—thought that lawyers and scientists, engineers and doctors can be unfeeling and insensitive people.

The highly deliberated can be thought of, then, as more compartmentalized and with a fairly static structure to their "organizational chart." The liberated may have looser links and boundaries between the different parts of their minds, leading to more communication and sometimes more chaos. Their reactions to the same situation will vary more than would those of the highly deliberated. One group would, if graphically represented, look like an airline meal, with all the different bits in isolated compartments; the other would look like a big stew in which a dash of any seasoning has an effect on everything in it. For deliberators, emotions, even highly felt ones, can be walled off from judgment or from their next job; for the liberated, feelings flow more freely over everything and color all.

On the other hand, the freer, liberated style lends itself to breakthroughs in creative thought. Creativity requires a thinker who doesn't follow the herd. In most cases, this means that one has lots of ideas that don't follow the usual sequences, which explains why many people who are thought to be highly creative are also considered unusual. Isaac Newton, for example, spent days locked in his room pouring over the mysteries of the Book of Daniel while he was working on the theory of gravity.

The eccentricity that seems to go with art, creative science, or writing can be expressed in either a high-gain or low-gain way. The painter Francis Bacon would get in the right frame of mind for work by staying up all hours, drinking and having sex as much as possible. Thus liberated, he would paint. Lower gain but just as liberated from convention, Albert Einstein, while sitting on a streetcar watching a clock tower recede, thought, If the streetcar were going at the speed of light, I'd see the same time on the clock face forever. Who would think that speed and time could be related in this way? Not anybody else who had come before him, deliberating along lines they had already soaked up.

Henri Matisse would paint the same painting over and over, wiping off the wet oil in the evening, until he made the right "spontaneous" move. The balance between deliberation and liberation may well involve more of the cerebral hemispheres as well as the frontal lobe alone.

Chapter 8

Positive Approach, Negative Withdrawal

*A*pproaching the world involves feeling positive toward it, while the signals for avoidance are negative feelings. The simplest judgment we make is whether anything is good or bad for us, whether an object or an event is positive or negative. When we feel something is positive, we feel able to approach, when we feel badly we tend to avoid or at least don't get any closer.

The decision to approach the good things and to withdraw from the bad is perhaps our most basic internal judgment of all. This dimension is found in decisions made by everything from bacteria up to go-go dancers and contains the basis for countless decisions we make about whether to move closer or to move away. Unlike with high or low gain and deliberation-liberation, we have fast access to this system; we sense this third continuum, approach-withdrawal, as our basic feeling tone.

Interestingly, these feelings also seem to be controlled by the frontal lobes, but differently in the left hemisphere and in the right. And the differences are present at birth. If how deliberate or liberated one is determines *whether* emotions will be freely expressed or controlled, the approach-avoidance system determines, in general, *which* emotions are part of our basic makeup.

A positive feeling like love or the taste of sweetness makes us want to draw or stay near. The smell of pie coming out of the oven, the warmth of the sun on a cold day, a smiling friend, or the appearance of a lover all deliver the signal "come closer, don't go away." Negative feelings such as anger, disgust, fear, anxiety, and the like signal the opposite: "avoid this, get out of here." We want to leave when a bear approaches us; when a car gets too close, we want to stop; we get away from a lamb chop covered in maggots.

Surprisingly much of our life is spent making these simple go-or-no-go, get-close-or-go-away decisions. They're involved in everything—the people we choose to live with, the people we pass in the street, the food we either eat or avoid. They determine the threats (as from charging tigers or approaching cars) or the benefits (appealing fruit, beckoning smiles) of objects while we navigate the world; they influence decisions about marriage, travel, the future, and so on. This dimension requires the least explication since we're all familiar with basing a judgment on "Is it good for me, or is it bad for me?" and "Do I like it or hate it?" The positive-negative continuum is immediately familiar to us all, much more so than are the other two dimensions.

It's not only a matter of feeling mostly good or bad, for psychologists have found positive affect and negative affect to be independent of one another.[1] This means that individuals can have either a lot of positive feelings, a lot of negative feelings, or both at the same time. We also know a bit about the areas of the brain that have an influence on these feelings. Differences in the asymmetry between the right and left hemispheres of the frontal lobes influence our basic feeling tone, and these differences show up early in life.

BACTERIA MAKING BASIC "GO/NO GO" DECISION—(APPROACH)

DANCER MAKING BASIC "GO-GO/NO GO-GO" DECISION—(AVOID)

Direction and Degree

There are basic differences in the direction and degree of emotional responsiveness that a person displays. When confronted with a spider, you might shriek and run from the room while your friend might calmly pick it up and place it outside.

---

1. The term *affect* refers to the feeling dimension of life. It is part of one's general outward emotional expression. Someone with a flat affect, for example, displays little or no emotion. The term *emotion* refers to a relatively specific pattern of short-lived physiological responses. Emotions arouse, communicate, direct, and sustain behavior. The term *feeling* refers to the subjective experience of emotions; feelings can be complex experiences, involving several different emotions at once. Finally, the term *mood* refers to a relatively long-lasting state of feeling. A mood sets the emotional backdrop for one's experience of the world.

Anyone can see that the tiniest babies show radically different approach and withdrawal tendencies, different levels of gregariousness and shyness. But infants can't tell us anything, and we can't do the physiological research on them that comparative psychologists perform on animals. It is a difficult question: how to study temperament and feelings in newborns.

In 1970, David Galin and I demonstrated that one can detect differences in which hemisphere is active at any moment by recording brain waves from each hemisphere and then comparing the amount of alpha rhythm occurring on each side at the same time. The alpha rhythm of the brain, a slow-wave smooth rhythm (eight to twelve hertz), signifies the idling of an area of the brain; faster, more jagged rhythms signify that the brain is involved in activity. Since then, others have investigated the relationship between approach or withdrawal emotions and activity in the two cerebral hemispheres.

In their intriguing series of studies, Davidson and colleagues showed that the left hemisphere may control different emotions from the right. The left seems to activate when a person experiences positive emotions, such as happiness, while the right hemisphere "lights up" when one endures negative emotions such as anger or disgust.

Davidson's basic experiment on adults worked this way: he asked people to recall times of great positive or negative feeling. When people were thinking about positive experiences, he found that the front of the left hemisphere was activated; when they were thinking negatively, the front of the right hemisphere lit up. Other scientists have confirmed this.

With his colleague Fox, Davidson tried to determine whether newborns have this reaction. The researchers gave newborns water followed by a sucrose solution and then by a citric acid solution (here's that lemon juice again!) while videotaping the babies' facial expressions. The researchers also recorded electroencephalograms (EEGs) from the frontal and parietal (2/3 of the way back) scalp regions on the left and right side. They found the same characteristic brain patterns that adults exhibit: activation of the left hemisphere in response to pleasure, activation of the right in response to disgust. This provides us with the best kind of evidence we are likely to get, since we have to use such young babies, that the two cerebral hemispheres of the brain are specialized at (or close to) birth for two different types of emotional experiences.

In another study, Davidson and Fox tested ten-month-old infants during the approach of their mother, a stranger, and during maternal separation. They found that when infants were approaching objects, touching them and making positive sounds or facial expressions of joy, there was greater relative left-frontal activity. During behaviors reflecting withdrawal, there was right-hemisphere activity. These effects seem to be quite localized to the frontal area.

Another study compared intervals of joy, anger, distress, disgust, and sadness and analyzed the EEGs during each period. Again, infants had greater left-hemisphere activity during joy and greater right-hemisphere activity during disgust and distress.

Then Davidson and Fox examined the prevalence of different emotions in newborns and recorded their EEGs, dividing those infants who displayed stress during separation from those who did not. The infants who displayed alpha rhythm in their right-hemisphere frontal lobes during separation—that is, the right hemisphere, associated with positive emotions, was less stimulated during this experience—were more likely to display distress and separation anxiety than the infants with less right-hemisphere alpha rhythm.

Why should this system be wired in this way? The left hemisphere, involved in positive feelings, also has control of the fine movements we make, such as those involved in sewing, writing, or typing. The right hemisphere, involved in negative feelings, controls the larger motor functions, such as the muscles involved in moving the legs or shoulders. One could surmise that it is efficient in terms of brain processes to have the "avoid" emotions located near the area that controls the muscles that do the avoiding, while the area that controls approaching movements lies close to the feelings that make one want to get close.

Three Temperament Dimensions

The three systems—high gain versus low gain, deliberation-liberation, and approach-withdrawal—give us a basis for analyzing differences in people. Certainly we can all recognize differences on the gain dimension—people who are constantly restless and yearning for new information versus those who seek peace and quiet. Differences on the deliberation-liberation dimension are familiar, too—some people have their lives, their day, even their lunch planned out, while others never get these things together but could make a major creative breakthrough in their work. And some people seem relentlessly sour, while others seem sunny no matter what.

No one remains at the same exact spot on any of these three continua. The most extreme low gainer sometimes has quiet moments at home, and high gainers may need some stimulation, even in the form of roller coasters or wild rafting rides. The most organized person gets loose and goofy once in a while, and the most free spirit may be able to balance a checkbook. But I believe these set points of an individual, like the set point of their weight, index different average positions over time on the dimensions of gain, deliberation-liberation, and approach-avoidance.

It's not fair to argue, "I'm supposed to be high gain, so how come I can do accounting?" A person who is usually heavy may weigh less when on a diet than a normally lighter person who's just spent a year in Paris. Over time, however, the set points prevail.

A further complication is that different people may have different margins of variability in the dimensions, much as they do in weight. A person with an average weight of 175 may slim down to 150 and go up to 200, while another at the same average weight may vary only five pounds from heaviest to thinnest. Thus some people move more than others from high to low gain, liberated to deliberated, approach to avoidance.

In the next chapter, we'll consider how, when each of these dimensions is taken to the extreme, characteristic disorders result. In later chapters, since there is certainly more to our individuality than just where we stand on each of these three dimensions, we'll consider other important roots of the self—how our family situation creates differences between our siblings and us, the nature of sex differences, the impact of our handedness, whether race makes a difference, and the differences in mental abilities that we inherit.

Chapter 9

Disorders

At the Ends of the Continuum

Each of us is neurotic in one sense or another. Each of us carries through life a set of unsolved problems, prejudices, and biases in response to our fellow human beings. Since neurosis so often disguises itself as normality and so often is indistinguishable from it, a major problem of adjustment is focused on the correct or incorrect diagnosis each of us makes of the other. The disorder in one life usually has repercussions in the lives of others, and that is the point. Normality, then, becomes a very relative term, and its limits are more elastic than most of us suspect. We are all, simultaneously, normal and abnormal.

ELTON MACNEIL, *THE QUIET FURIES*

*E*ach of us moves up and down around a point on the three continua of self—gain, deliberation-liberation, and approach/withdrawal. For some who are closer to the ends of one of these continua, more difficulties ensue, difficulties we still call neurotic. And at the extremes of the continua, there are severe disturbances, especially of mood and of the degree of organization of behaviors. These severe disturbances are what we will concentrate on here.

Of course, external circumstances affect us as well. In everyone's life there are times of extreme stress when one is less able to cope with the problems of living. Violence and riots occur more during heat waves, for example, and there are more admissions to

At extremes, disorder ensues

mental hospitals during recessions and other times of economic hardship.

Part of the differences is this: everybody does crazy things sometimes, but normally the order in life returns. When one finds it impossible to return to an acceptable level of control over one's daily life, then one may need to seek help. It is like the difference between a brief bout with the flu and a chronic illness, a matter of degree. Normally, one would be saddened and would probably cry when a love affair ends or when a parent dies. However, it becomes an affliction if you are so disturbed that for three years afterward you cannot go to a party. And it is one thing to be anxious about going to a party and another to be so afraid of meeting people that you cannot go outside your house at all.

Just as people may have a "touch of the flu," they may have a touch of the disorders at either end of each continuum, such as a tendency to go to emotional extremes or to seek sensation recklessly. If high sensation seeking becomes recklessness and then is combined with a lack of emotional recognizance and the wrong milieu, it may enhance a tendency toward criminality. A chronic negative mood can shade into depression. A high degree of organization can become meticulousness, or obsessiveness, or, at the far end, obsessive-compulsive disorder (OCD).

Obsession can reach pathological proportions, and the compulsive routines which can develop hamper the ordinary life of an individual. One such individual was Malcolm. He became obsessed with his teeth, and would stand brushing them compulsively, for longer and longer each day—examining his teeth very carefully, scrubbing and brushing them methodically, going over and over each tooth again and again. As the length of the ritual extended, he would have to get up earlier and earlier, so that he could take the time he needed for tooth brushing before going to work. He would get up at six A.M., then five A.M., then four A.M., until finally he had to stop going to work at all. At this point a psychiatrist began treating him for his compulsions. Not everyone becomes obsessive so gradually, some people just snap and can't stop worrying about their actions.

At the other end, liberation might begin with a delightful openness to experience, enhanced creativity, then to "ditziness" in someone who is never on time, or can't organize their life routines, someone who loses keys, directions, who tends to "space out," and who is often confused. Further on the continuum lies schizo-typal tendencies and schizophrenia.

Whether one has a disorder of the self is a delicate question since the "dividing line" between normal and abnormal is not absolute. Conceptions of normality change with the times, and disorder is often in the eye of the observer. A century ago it would have been considered abnormal for a woman to have premarital sex, and she might have been locked away for it. Now it is not. Homosexuality used to be classified as a disorder; now it is not. Cultures change and standards change.

Yet anyone who has worked with psychotics in a mental hospital or in another setting knows that severe disorders aren't just a matter of definition or preference. Contrary to the romantic view of psychiatrist R. D. Laing, who held that schizophrenia was actually a breakthrough in consciousness that could lead to a new way of understanding life, many people have genuine and severe difficulty in comprehending the world and organizing their actions. Break*down* is much more like it, unfortunately. Such people are in real need of help.

But how can such bizarre phenomena as believing one is Jesus Christ, or hearing voices, or cleaning the room 250 times per day simply be extensions of our normal activities? They seem so different from, so discontinuous with the norm. Let's think about what happens when an ordinary continuum is extended. One woman drives around a curve in the road at forty miles per hour, which might be safe. Another drives at forty-five, and although this speed makes the car a little skiddy and more difficult to control, she is also unharmed. A third drives at sixty, which is only a little higher on the speed continuum, but she finds herself in a completely different state: off the road, over a cliff, needing hospitalization. At the extremes of a continuum, the state changes. It is akin to the difference between a frog in 210-degree water and one in 212-degree water. At 210 degrees, the frog is hot; at 212 degrees, the poor frog is boiled. Let's now look at what happens at similar break points in the three continua.

*B*ecause the brain's mechanisms for adaptation can be overwhelmed by too much change, challenge, and stress, people often become ill after experiencing major changes such as

Extremes of Gain: Anxiety and Arousal

marriage, a vacation, marital separation, the death of a close friend, and the like. Psychologists analyze these "life events" as if everybody responds to them in the same way. However, as we have seen, individuals differ in their level of arousal and need for stimulation, change, and conflict. Some love the tumult and stress of uncertainty, while others are so internally aroused that they need a quiet, calm world outside. For the latter, lots of clutter and change in their lives can overwhelm them.

Highly introverted people, the high gainers, often find that arousal amplifies their worries. Thus, anxiety disorders are at one end of the gain continuum.

People suffering from high anxiety live with constant tension and worry. They seem uneasy when they are around people and are unusually sensitive to comments and criticisms. Often they are so terrified of making a mistake that they cannot concentrate or make decisions. Their posture is often strained and rigid, resulting in sore muscles (especially in the neck and shoulders). They may have chronic insomnia and gastrointestinal problems (such as diarrhea), perspire heavily, and experience high blood pressure, heart palpitations, and breathlessness. Regardless of how well things are actually going, they are always worried that something will go wrong.

High arousal problems often result in high anxiety, which affects about 3 percent of the population. The association between high internal anxiety and the quietness observable to others is most strong in catatonics with stupor, where the arousal is so high that the person simply shuts off completely. In catatonia with stupor, a person might maintain a single posture for days, usually one that a normal person would find difficult to maintain for more than a few minutes. One such woman explained that the reason she held her arm in front of her, palm outstretched, was that the forces of good and evil were warring on the palm of her hand and she did not want to upset the balance in favor of evil. Catatonia is often not a matter of internal emptiness but an extreme reaction to overload.

When I was in college, I worked three nights a week and during the day on Saturdays and Sundays as a psychiatric aide in a mental hospital in New York City. On my first day, I went into the room of Jack L., a catatonic in stupor, and was supposed to go into the closet to get him a new set of clothes. But the latch on the closet was old-fashioned and I couldn't get it open. I went back for the supervisor, but he wasn't around. I returned to the room, and Jack L., who was still rigid, still immobile when I came in, suddenly relaxed and said, "You have to give it a turn to the left, then press down." He went back to his pose. For the next two years, I never heard anything else from him, but he had noticed that I was new, and he knew what I wanted to know, probably because others had cursed the latch before.

All the time I worked in this hospital I also didn't understand why, during the "drug time," the boisterous hysterics would drop like flies when they got their tranquilizers, while the catatonics, "cats" as we called them, didn't get drowsy even under heavy sedation. It's again an example of the reversal that those being internally highly aroused are quiet, those internally low gain act boisterously.

The gain dimension extends from hysteria at one end to dysthymia (a long-lasting, apathetic, dulled, dampened-down frame of mind) at the other. Dysthymia also affects about 3 percent of the population. And the dysthymics are very, very difficult to sedate.

The most common disorders involve extremes of feelings. Consider this manic woman:

Approach and Withdrawal 1: Extremes of Feeling

You look like a couple of bright, alert, hard working, clean-cut, energetic, go-getters, and I could use you in my organization! I need guys that are loyal and enthusiastic about the great opportunities life offers on this planet! It's yours for the taking! Too many people pass opportunity by without hearing it knock because they don't know how to grasp the moment and strike while the iron is hot! You've got to grab it when it comes up for air, pick up the ball and run! You've got to be decisive! decisive! decisive! No shilly-shallying! Sweat! Yeah, sweat with a goal! Push, push, push, and you can push over a mountain! Two mountains, maybe. It's not luck! Hell, if it wasn't for bad luck I wouldn't have any luck at all! Be there firstest with the mostest! My guts and your blood! That's the system! I know, you know, he, she, or it knows it's the only way to travel! Get 'em off balance, baby, and the rest is leverage! Use your head and save your heels! What's this deal? Who are these guys? Have you got a telephone and a secretary I could

have instanter if not sooner? What I need is office space and the old
LDO [long-distance operator].

ELTON MACNEIL, *THE QUIET FURIES*

At the extremes of the approach-withdrawal continuum lie
elation, depression, and their combination. These emotional (or af-
fective) disorders afflict 5 to 8 percent of all people at some time in
their lives. Of these people, 6 percent of the women and 3 percent
of the men have an episode serious enough to require hospitalization. When the episode involves behavior at the elated, excited
end of the continuum, it is called mania.

People with mania often experience elevated moods as pure
euphoria, and anyone who knows such a person can recognize that
the euphoria is a bit excessive. Manic people seem to be "not themselves." The happiness has no specific cause and is not under the
person's control.

While most of us live near the center of the approach-withdrawal spectrum, the manic person has unbounded enthusiasm for
everyone and everything. The two characteristic qualities of euphoria and expansiveness, if not too extreme, can be infectious,
but when a person approaches, grabs, and tries to manipulate
everything, he or she may require hospitalization.

At the other end of the continuum is depression, when one
withdraws from and avoids everything, where nothing seems of
any value and one's mind becomes filled with negative thoughts
about one's life. Depression has been referred to as the "common
cold" of disorders. We often use the word *depressed* to mean sad,
upset, or in a bad mood. "I'm depressed—we lost the IBM con-
tract," a businessperson might say. But clinical depression is much
more than a down mood. It is a severe mental disorder that results
in an overwhelming, immobilizing sadness, arresting the entire
course of a person's life. Here is Martin Seligman's description of
a college student suffering from severe depression:

Nancy entered the university with a superb high school record. She had
been president and salutatorian of her class, and a popular and pretty
cheerleader. Everything she wanted had always fallen into her lap;
good grades came easily and boys fell over themselves competing for
her attentions. She was an only child, and her parents doted on her,

rushing to fulfill her every whim; her successes were their triumphs, her failures their agony. Her friends nicknamed her Golden Girl. When I met her in her sophomore year, she was no longer a Golden Girl. She said that she felt empty, that nothing touched her any more; her classes were boring and the whole academic system seemed an oppressive conspiracy to stifle her creativity. The previous semester she had received two F's. She had "made it" with a succession of young men, and was currently living with a dropout. She felt exploited and worthless after each sexual adventure; her current relationship was on the rocks, and she felt little but contempt for him and for herself. She had used soft drugs extensively and had once enjoyed being carried away on them. But now even drugs had lost their appeal. She was majoring in philosophy, and had a marked emotional attraction to Existentialism: like the existentialists, she believed that life is absurd and that people must create their own meaning. This belief filled her with despair. Her despair increased when she perceived her own attempts to create meaning—participation in the movements for women's liberation and against the war in Vietnam—as fruitless. When I reminded her that she had been a talented student and was still an attractive and valuable human being, she burst into tears: "I fooled you, too."

MARTIN SELIGMAN, *LEARNED HELPLESSNESS*

There are two kinds of severe depressive disorders. In *unipolar* depression, an individual suffers only from depression, while in *bipolar* depression, a person suffers from depression as well as mania. An individual in a manic episode is in a frenzy of overexcitability and activity. The happiness is as out of control as is the sadness of the depression, and the swing between the two often leads to hospitalization.

The current diagnosis for depression includes loss of interest and pleasure, even with friends and family. Appetite and sleep are disturbed. There's often a lot of agitation; depressives may pull their hair, pace up and down, and wring their hands. They feel consistently tired, although they have done nothing physically taxing. The prospect of having to do even the smallest task is overwhelming. And this can lead to an overwhelming feeling of worthlessness.

Bipolar depression affects about 1 percent of the population. While women are more likely than men to suffer from unipolar depression, there is no sex difference in the bipolar form, and it can occur at any age. A "bipolar" person often experiences his or her first manic episode before the age of thirty.

Both forms of the disorder have a genetic component. Studies of identical twins find an extremely high relationship. If one twin has bipolar disorder, the likelihood that the other twin will have it is 72 percent; for fraternal twins, the likelihood is 14 percent. In unipolar disorder, the likelihood is 40 percent for identical twins but only 11 percent for fraternal twins.

Life circumstances, of course, do affect depression. Depressed patients report two to three times as many disruptive events, like losing a job, occurring just before a depression. Marital separation increases the probability of depression by a factor of five to six; still, fewer than 10 percent of those who separate from their spouse become clinically depressed.

One consistent difference, nonetheless, is that unipolar depression appears twice as often in women as it does in men. Why? Some researchers argue that the hormonal fluctuations associated with the menstrual cycle make women more vulnerable to clinical depression. However, while women are more likely to be depressed after the birth of a child, most of those so depressed were also depressed before the child was born.

It is more likely that the reason resides in the fact that some women defer to men in decisions about careers, about where the family lives, and even about minor day-to-day choices. Thus, some women may begin to believe that they have little control over the world around them, and they may, therefore, feel helpless. Learned helplessness is a powerful predictor of clinical depression.

Women's traditional roles do not place them at risk for all psychological disorders; men, on the other hand, suffer disproportionately higher rates than women of alcohol and drug abuse, hyperactivity, and antisocial personality disorder. However, it does appear that women respond differently than men do to despair. And this may be another reason that they are more likely to become clinically depressed.

Perhaps the way that males and females respond to despondency is the cause of the depression. Psychologist Susan Nolen-Hoeksema observes that males contest the beginning of depression by doing a lot of new or pleasurable things, which may distract them from their mood. The more empathetic women focus on the mood itself and, in doing so, amplify it.

If males and females do indeed respond differently to distress—and as a result show different rates of various disorders—then each sex has something to learn from the other. Diversion may help to insulate a person from despair, but if used excessively, it may place him or her at risk for other psychopathology, such as antisocial personality disorder. Similarly, focusing on feelings may be very useful at times, but in excess it may lead to clinical depression.

Approach and Withdrawal 2: Antisocial Personality

*N*ot all people suffer from an excess of feelings; some suffer from a *lack* of emotional responsivity. Such people are classified as "antisocial" or, as it used to be called, "psychopathic." They are capable of using people and toying with others' emotions. They may be "confidence men" or women, exploiting others for sex or money with no feelings of guilt. Or they may be our all-too-familiar modern corporate amoral type, making money, making their way, or making love without concern.

There is evidence that genetic factors contribute to antisocial personality. Children of criminal fathers have a less reactive autonomic nervous system (ANS) (the involuntary component of emotional responses) response than do children of noncriminals. In a study of hundreds of boys, George Wadsworth noted the pulse rate of eleven-year-olds just before a mild stress. He compared these to their pulse rates under stress and to later records of delinquency. Those with low increases in pulse rate under stress were much more likely to become delinquent. Also, biological relatives of adopted criminals have a higher rate of criminality and antisocial behavior than does the general population. In studies of the antisocial personality, the same relationship holds: the transmission from the biological father is significant.

Why does criminality run in families? Most of this influence has to do with the milieu, but there are ANS differences as well. Individuals differ in their responsiveness to punishment. What might be inherited, then, is an emotional reactivity that is less responsive than the norm, so that when these individuals are punished for transgressions, they don't much *feel* it. This lessened feeling can underlie mental disorders. When, in addition, the young mind is exposed to a violent world, then the mind grows up to represent the entire world as a violent place. This combination can lead to deficiencies in learning law-abiding behavior, to less responsiveness to others' feelings, and to the need to create excitement. These are all characteristics of the antisocial personality.

Most people experience a good deal of emotional arousal both before and after they commit a transgression. We feel our heart beating, for instance, when we are about to do something bad. But either this does not happen to sociopathic criminals or they do not recognize their body signals in the same way. Stanley Schachter and Bibb Latane conducted a research program that compared prison inmates who had been diagnosed as sociopathic with other inmates who were not sociopaths. They found that it's not only that sociopaths don't get so aroused but that sometimes when they do experience the same physiological arousal as nonsociopathic prisoners, they don't connect their racing heartbeat or quickness of breath with the punishment. They are cut off from this common means of learning not to do something wrong again.

This research is supported by the fact that sociopathic prisoners are much less likely to learn how to solve a problem and how to avoid electric shocks. Before committing emotional crimes, people usually become physiologically aroused and apply some kind of label like passion, jealousy, or hatred to their arousal. Sociopaths don't connect the physiological arousal to emotions, and they rarely commit crimes of passion, such as murder, rape, and assault. But sociopathic criminals do engage in a very high proportion of the nonemotional crimes, like burglary, forgery, and con games.

Again, while all crimes can't be explained, perhaps some of us have a predisposition to ignore social norms and other people's feelings. Perhaps some of the roots of some types of criminality, then, lie at the extremes of the approach-withdrawal dimension, where we also find depression, mania, and their combination.

Deliberation-Liberation 1: Obsessive-Compulsive Disorder

*W*hile emotions are basic to our judgments, keeping our actions and the information in the world regulated are important to our sense of self. When individuals go to the extremes of the deliberation-liberation continuum, we find a couple of the most serious disorders.

We constantly check what we do. And we worry about things like: Did I leave the iron on? Is the side door locked? Do the cats have food? Are my clothes clean? We aim our cars so as to avoid hitting curbs or, worse, people, and if we come too close, we may check the mirror. The frontal lobes participate in this process of checking actions.

People, of course, "normally" differ on this dimension quite widely, as we saw in Chapter Seven. I have a friend, for example, who leaves his house open when he's away so that his friends can get in. He encourages us to eat and drink anything, and if we don't clean up, he will get the maid to do it. (His name is available for a small fee.) Another good friend has a weekend cabin on the door of which he has posted a list of the more than two hundred things to check in the house. The list notes the exact position of the gas switch, the number of boxes of corn flakes on the shelves, the amount of water that should be in the tank. Even his own family has to go through the checking routine—check for the item, then check it off the list.

Circumstances can change our individual settings on what we might call our "worry circuit," sometimes causing us to move further out on the continuum. When I go to the airport for a foreign flight, for instance, I check my passport and tickets again and again, even though I have a travel jacket with a zippered pocket in which I usually put them. Surely, if the passport and the tickets were in the pocket when I left the house, they'd still be there ten minutes later. But I check anyway. And often, just half an hour later when I've parked in the airport garage, I slap my pocket once more just to be sure that I feel their comforting presence.

In some people, however, the control of the worry circuit breaks down, and the normal reassurance that shuts off the circuit is never received.

> I'm driving down the highway doing 55 MPH. I'm on my way to take a final exam. My seat belt is buckled and I'm vigilantly following all the rules of the road. No one is on the highway—not a living soul. Out of nowhere an Obsessive-Compulsive Disorder (OCD) attack strikes. It's almost magical the way it distorts my perception of reality. While in reality no one is on the road, I'm intruded with the heinous thought that I might have hit someone . . . a human being! God knows where such a fantasy comes from. I think about this for a second and then say to myself, "That's ridiculous. I didn't hit anybody." Nonetheless, a

gnawing anxiety is born. An anxiety I will ultimately not be able to put away until an enormous price has been paid. . . . The pain is a terrible guilt that I have committed an unthinkable, negligent act. At one level, I know this is ridiculous, but there's a terrible pain in my stomach telling me something quite different. . . . I start ruminating, "Maybe I did hit someone and didn't realize it. . . . Oh, my God! I might have killed somebody! I have to go back and check. . . ." I've driven five miles farther down the road since the attack's onset. I turn the car around and head back to the scene of the mythical mishap.

JUDITH RAPPAPORT, *THE BOY WHO COULDN'T STOP WASHING*

Washing hands constantly, being fearful of touching things because they could be dirty, taking all day to get dressed because each step must be taken in a certain order with a certain thoroughness, worrying that you have killed someone on the road (and feeling satisfied only when you drive back to check), saving everything, counting things endlessly—these are symptoms of obsessive-compulsive disorder.

OCD may seem bizarre to people without the disorder. However, it is simply an extreme version of normal behavior. The common fixations of OCD concern health and safety behaviors that we learn as children—to be clean, neat, and careful. If you touch something filthy, you may not be fully at ease until you have thoroughly washed your hands. You might have a well-defined morning ritual that prepares you to face the world, and if you leave out a step, say, putting on your dress, or shaving, you are likely to feel somewhat uncomfortable for a part of the day. And normal caution on the highway requires that you take care not to hit anything, especially not fellow human beings.

OCD reveals something about how the brain's worry circuit helps ensure that important actions are completed.

The frontal lobes and associated structures, all key parts of the deliberation-liberation system, are the areas involved in OCD. One small structure, the caudate nucleus, filters the flood of anxious feelings and sensations from the orbitofrontal cortex (which is located just above the eyes) and relays only the significant worries to the thalamus for further action. However, in someone with OCD, as neuroscientist Lewis Baxter told *Time* magazine, the caudate nucleus is "a poor executive officer. He's bombarded with messages from worrywarts. But instead of setting priorities, he gets excited about all the messages and passes them on to the dispatcher."

A similar interpretation of the findings by Thomas Insel of the National Institutes of Mental Health Laboratory of Neurophysiology is that OCD sufferers become unable to resist compulsions arising from the worry system because of abnormal neural activity within the system. PET scans of brains of people with OCD show that when one part of the worry loop is active, all other parts of the system are active also. After successful treatment, there is no longer such a strong connection among all the brain centers involved. Treatment either suppresses activity in some brain centers, or increases it in others, or both in order to restore balance.

People with OCD appear to act in response to internal cues—that is, obsessions. They may have to expend extra mental effort to suppress compulsive behaviors, which would account for the increases in the activity of the orbitofrontal cortex observed in their brains. Letting down the struggle to hold back compulsive behavior may mean decreasing activity in this brain area, and this may result in increased impulsive behavior.

One of the strongest indications that the frontal cortex might act to keep a lid on obsessions comes from the case of Evan, who was studied by neurologist Antonio Damasio. Evan was the oldest of five children. By age twenty-five, he was a staff accountant and the father of two. For ten more years, things went well, including promotions and other life successes. But his personality changed dramatically following surgery to remove a tumor from his orbitofrontal cortex. After the surgery, he began to have visual and behavioral problems.

A tumor on the surface of the cortex, called a meningioma, pressed on the brain. During surgery, Evan lost much of the frontal cortex. Now, in contrast to his previous life, Evan began to make mistakes. He got into shady business deals. He lost his life savings. He lost his job, and then his marriage broke up as well. He moved back home in defeat.

What had gone wrong? His intellectual ability, in the narrow sense, was fine, but he couldn't make good decisions, and he obsessed over small matters. He needed two hours to get ready for work in the morning and spent much of the day shaving and washing his hair. He'd spend a lot of time deciding where to dine each night, trying to figure out each restaurant's seating plan, as well as other particulars such as the menu, atmosphere, and management. He would drive to each restaurant to see how busy it was, but even then he could not finally decide which one to choose. He kept everything, even long-dead house plants and old phone books; he had six out-of-order fans, five broken television sets, three bags full of empty orange-juice-concentrate cans, fifteen cigarette lighters, and countless stacks of old newspapers.

Without the part of the frontal cortex that Evan had lost, he just wasn't able to finish the process of making a decision, such as when to throw something out or when to stop weighing the merits of a restaurant and just go in and eat, at least before they all close.

The OCD brain condition is not beyond hope, however. Both drug and behavior treatments have proved effective in reducing OCD symptoms. Behavior therapy consists primarily of exposure to the stimulus that tends to evoke compulsive behavior, such as dirt, and when the horrible consequences don't follow, the worry circuit quiets down, the strange behaviors become less frequent, and there is evidence that the brain physiology changes as well. Drug therapies can produce similar results; the checking circuit returns to a normal range of operation, and excessive deliberations cease.

Deliberation-Liberation 2: Schizophrenia

*I*ndividuals who are at the other end of the deliberation-liberation continuum are highly disorganized, instead of exceedingly organized. For the most part, they suffer from a weakened regulation of information and actions. They hardly have the worries of someone with OCD, but they have a different deficiency: a disordered structure to perceptions and to the control of their actions. Whimsy can be wonderful, but not as a way to run one's whole life, as it was for Meriel.

Consider how we normally regulate the flow of information. The mind works so fast and so constantly that we're usually unconscious of this process. The outside world is full of information about all sorts of events—whether it's raining, whether someone is speaking English or a language unknown to us, whether the sounds we hear are threatening, what our needs are, what kind of emotional mood we're in. Our mental system simplifies and selects, filters and interprets all this information.

Normally we filter out the irrelevant. The next time you are at a party, note how easily you can listen to the person speaking to you, even though there is a lot of other talk going on. As an experiment, try, without being too impolite, to "tune in" one of the other conversations in the background. You will see that you can do this easily, simply by switching your filtering of the information. This happens automatically when someone mentions your name or says something shocking. In this way, we keep track of what's going on around us and tune in and out of what's central to us. This focusing of attention allows us to direct our actions.

Most of this process is automatic: individual sounds become higher-order concepts, like words, through the instantaneous interpretation of our brain. Sometimes we instantly overinterpret the shards of sounds we all hear, such as random noises and fragments of conversations, and experience them, thus constructed, as meaningful. When we have a problem doing so, our functioning may become disordered.

An office worker who is beginning to go deaf but doesn't know it will unconsciously "fill in" what he fails to hear and continue about his job. But he may "hear"—that is, interpret—the wrong thing and thus may begin to make mistakes. Similarly, none of us can possibly perceive everything that goes on outside us; there simply isn't time. So we fill in the blanks in much the same way, constructing a representation of the world as we go.

Suppose you have failing hearing and do not know it. You may think that others are whispering in your presence. Our normal perceptual mechanisms interpret sensory input in the simplest meaningful way, so you would probably decide that people are whispering because they do not want you to hear them. Perhaps you interpret this to mean that they do not like you, or that they are conspiring against you, or that they plan to exclude you from some activity. A condition known as *sensory paranoia* may result from this kind of interpretation of faulty information, as can schizophrenia. The following excerpt provides an extreme example:

After supper, I sat quietly in the day room trying to watch TV. The medication was slowing me down considerably, and even the simplest movement seemed to take forever.

The voices gathered behind me, keeping up a running commentary on everything that was happening.

A nurse breezed through the day room on her way down another hallway. "There goes the nurse," said a voice.

A flash of light zoomed across the day room, burning out and disappearing into thin air. Had I really seen that?

"There goes another comet," said a voice.

Okay, I did see it. This could mean only one thing: further leakage of the Other Worlds into this world. The comet had been a sign.

"It's all right," Hal reassured me with his sugary voice. "We're here with you."

Interference Patterns began to materialize in the air. I stared at their colorful swirls, watching new patterns emerge in response to every sound in the room. When the voices spoke, the patterns shifted, just as they did with other sounds. It was like the vampire test: vampires don't have reflections in mirrors; nonexistent voices shouldn't affect the patterns the way other sounds did. That was scientific proof that the voices were just as real as everything else in the world; actually they seemed even more real.

Frightening. I didn't know whether existence in the Other World would be divinely magnificent, beyond human description, like heaven, or whether it would be like the worst imaginable hell. I was ambivalent about whether I wanted it to happen. On the one hand, I didn't want to stop the emergence of goodness, yet if it threatened to be hellish, I would have to try to prevent it. I froze, not wanting to produce further patterns from the stimulation of my bodily movement. I didn't want to be responsible for encouraging such change in the world. Live your life as a prayer, I reminded myself. I heard a news announcer on TV parrot my words: "Live your life as a prayer."

Yes, that was good advice for the world to know. The newscaster had broadcast my own thought. The communication systems brought in from the Other Worlds were incredibly sophisticated, more than I could understand. The whole world was now praying with me. A nurse sat down next to me on the couch and put her hand on my arm. "Carol, what's going on with you? You're just sitting there doing nothing. Are you bored?"

The sound of her voice created new waves of Interference Patterns, sent hurtling through the air in front of us.

Hush! Don't you understand what you're doing? For God's sake, don't help the Other Side.

She shook my arm gently. "Why, Carol, I believe you look scared. Am I right?"

Oh, no, now you've done it, you've inadvertently hurled us into that bottomless pit. With the force of your movement you've made us start to fall again.

The nurse got up and went for help. She returned with two male aides, who picked me up off the couch, carried me to my bed, and left me lying there alone in the dark. The whole time, the patterns swirled through the air, crashing over my head like a tidal wave. Would any of us survive this ordeal?

On my bed, undisturbed, unmoving, I applied the powers of my concentration, gradually settling the turbulent waters of the Other Side. The Interference Patterns began to fade back into the air. If I could only lie still indefinitely, I might have a chance.

CAROL NORTH, *WELCOME, SILENCE*

One woman who suffered a similar episode later became a psychiatric nurse. She writes, "I had very little ability to sort the relevant from the irrelevant. The filter had broken down. Completely unrelated events became intricately connected in my mind." These attentional deficiencies often occur before the onset of the episode.

While "schizophrenia" isn't anywhere near as precise a diagnosis as is OCD, it is the name for a group of disorders that involve severe disorganization of one's mental abilities. While mild disorganization may well liberate the individual from rigid methods of doing things, this fundamental disorganization causes disturbances in every area of life: social functioning, feelings, and behavior.

There are common thought disturbances that go with schizophrenia. Schizophrenic people often have the delusion that someone is spying on them. Often they give inappropriate, unusual, or impossible significance to events. One man was convinced that

Ronald Reagan was instructing him on one of his television broadcasts. Other delusions include *thought broadcast,* the belief that others hear one's thoughts; *thought insertion,* the belief that others are inserting thoughts into one's mind; *thought withdrawal,* the sensation that one's thoughts are being stolen from one's mind; and *delusions of being controlled,* the belief that one's actions and thoughts are being controlled by outside forces.

The form of one's thoughts is disturbed as well; there is a loosening of associations, and ideas shift from one topic to another with no apparent connections. Auditory hallucinations ("voices") are common, although visual and olfactory ones may also occur. Feelings are blunted; the sense of self is distorted.

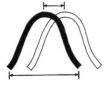

What possible adaptation could there be in schizophrenia? Not much to the person suffering from the disorder, I'm afraid. Let's take a wider view and consider schizophrenics as the extreme of a continuum of people, and then consider the advantage that individuals close to the schizophrenic might have.

First, there is some correlation between being gifted and socially prominent and being a *relative of a schizophrenic.* Such people often achieve great success in science, art, or the pursuit of power. Geneticist John Karlsson, using data from his native Iceland, found a great number of schizophrenics in close biological relationships to people who were outstandingly creative. This would suggest that the genes responsible for the roots of schizophrenia also underlie some creative ability. Those getting a little of the liberation and openness on this end of the continuum may benefit society in their ability to make unforeseen connections, while those with too much may become disorganized beyond repair.

For instance, if you assemble a bicycle seat and handlebars so that the handlebars project over the thick end of the seat and thus produce an abstracted sculptural representation of a bull, you'd be Picasso. But if you decided to chop up a bicycle seat and handlebars to use for hamburger, you'd be nuts.

OCD can be thought of as a highly deliberated restriction of thought, and it is sometimes called overexclusive. It limits thought to one subject, such as "Did I hit someone?" Some forms of schizophrenia represent, in contrast, an unwanted liberation—an opening of the gates—a condition sometimes called overinclusive. Some schizophrenics, then, have difficulty limiting the content of their consciousness, and consequently they misconstrue the information they receive.

In addition, in schizophrenics, there just isn't a separation among different perceived items or even between themselves and the world. The feeling of skinlessness experienced by those with weak boundaries, mentioned in Chapter Seven, occurs again and again. Sylvia Plath wrote in *The Bell Jar*, "It's as if neither of us or especially myself had any skin." This sense of skinlessness, leaving one feeling like an open channel to the world, seems central to the schizophrenic experience. When there is no deliberation, then information flows inward unimpeded and too often unrestrained. Plath said, "I'm afraid. I am not solid, but hollow. I feel behind my eyes a numb, paralyzed cavern, a pit of hell, nothingness."

One psychiatrist describes the fairy-tale writer Hans Christian Andersen in this way:

> His main interest was in his little puppet theatre, and this is where he began to create his stories. . . . His "skinlessness" was only too obvious. . . . His own reason he gave for his survival was that he was supremely capable of withdrawing into fantasy away from actual reality, thus transforming an unkind and often belligerent world into a fairy story.

Gordon Claridge has contributed much information and insight on what is common to the mind of schizophrenics and to that of others close to them on my deliberation-liberation continuum. If schizophrenia involves a failure to limit the contents of consciousness, then do all individuals differ on how much irrelevant information intrudes into consciousness? The answer seems to be yes.

Classified close to schizophrenics are "schizotypal" individuals, who evidence magical thinking, are often isolated socially, have repeated illusions, suspicions, latent paranoia, and some social anxiety. Yet a number of studies have shown that schizotypals are much more aware of what is going on in their minds than are others. They have a much greater richness of association, which again in a mild form can lead to creativity—or to a total breakdown and incoherence, when the inhibitions are removed.

Claridge's insight is that some individuals with this disorder lack the ordinary deliberation in the early stages of their sensory information processing and this leads to much variability in the information that reaches consciousness. In this view, schizophrenic symptoms (voices, paranoia, and so on) are due to a misinterpretation of the flood of information; in schizophrenics, the background sounds that we all hear in a crowd or in a room decode into voices telling the person what to do.

Claridge's initial studies discovered that schizophrenics and schizotypals find irrelevant material intruding into their consciousness. This is good evidence that the delusions result from the brain trying to make sense of this irrelevant information. He then set up an experiment to further test this phenomenon, using the "negative priming effect." In this experiment, a person looked at a screen onto which a number of symbols were being flashed; the person was instructed to ignore all but one type—the target symbol. The rest of the symbols were distractor symbols. Normally, people who are exposed to such conflicting information do worse than those not exposed, since they are distracted.

If one of the distractor symbols then became the target symbol, most subjects responded more slowly to the new target than they did if the new target were completely unfamiliar. This is because the subjects had already trained themselves to ignore the distractor symbol, and it would take a while for them to reverse the action of their regulatory filter. In schizophrenics, this doesn't happen, since they can't control their "filter." Since the problem is with regulating their input, this would cause a lot of unregulated information coming in to consciousness, and the person is, essentially always distracted, thus, the negative priming effect was much weaker.

Claridge also found that high schizotypals prime more slowly than normals on a word presentation experiment. They are more variable, too; they allow more influences into consciousness, so distractions aren't so distracting since there is no deliberate order to the events coming in. Their filters are more open to experiences and thoughts as well. This study provides some of the first direct evidence that disorganization and increased variability of the information entering the brain may play a role in schizotypal thought and in some schizophrenia.

In individuals closer to the middle of the deliberation-liberation continuum, we may find that this increased variability in the amount of information received will strongly influence their lives.

If someone has a nervous system that takes in a variable amount of information, this may well manifest itself in unstable thoughts and judgment, whimsy, or perhaps a bit of impulsivity. In other words, people who suddenly have different emotional readings of their marriage or relationships, who completely "change their minds" even after thinking a course of action through, may do so because of variations in their information flow; this amounts to a sort of 10 percent schizophrenia. And the manifestations of that variable information may well become these people's dominant characteristics, as they did for Meriel.

This way of thinking about order and disorder is bound to cause some debate, so I wish to reiterate that the idea of the three continua is a theory of a description of *different individuals,* not of process that exists inside one person. While any one individual might at different times vary somewhat from his or her "set point" and become more or less emotional or more or less arousable, the extremes like OCD, mania, and schizophrenia are true discontinuous breakdowns.

Anyone, not just deliberators, can have the "worry circuit" fracture in his or her caudate and thus become more likely to suffer from OCD. However, it's no coincidence, in this viewpoint, that the circuit in question is part of the frontal lobe–limbic system, which underlies the organization of our actions. It isn't in the parietal lobes or in the central areas of the cortex. But if you're like my friend who lists two hundred items to check at his house for the weekend, you're probably no more likely to have OCD than my other more "liberated" open-house friend. The continuum is a way to comprehend different people along consistent dimensions, and it might well help to make sense of the relationship between order and disorder and the underlying brain mechanisms.

Part Three

Race, Sex, and Family

Chapter 10

Skin Color, Cultural Differences, Cultural Practices, and Individuality

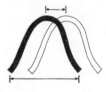

While temperament influences everything we do, it isn't the only influence on us. We are a mixture of independent influences, each one having nothing to do with the other. Whether we're of black or white skin color has nothing to do with whether we're first- or secondborn or whether our parents divorce or not, and neither of these factors has anything to do with whether we're right- or left-handed. Yet each of these factors independently contributes to who we are. This section considers some of the most evident differences among individuals: matters of race, of family, and of sex.

One can't look at any crowd without noticing how very diverse a bunch is humanity. Adults can vary in height from under four feet to around eight, in hair color from light blond or white to jet black, in eye color from pale blue to dark brown, in weight from seventy pounds to over a thousand. We have different size noses, our hearts differ in the way they branch and the rate at which they beat, our stomachs don't look like each others'. We vary in sex, of course, in which hand we prefer to use for writing and drawing, and in which eye is dominant. Our brains vary, too; they are as different as are our faces. But

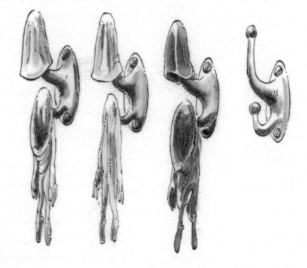

Skin color isn't more relevant than our clothes' color

which of these differences helps us to know our individual self? Which ones matter?

Skin color is one of the most obvious differences among people. After all, the skin is what we see of ourselves and others. Because it is so visible, so obvious, and so extensive, skin color takes on a prime position in our understanding of ourselves and others. Thus, when we hear that a people of one skin color are especially intelligent or that those of another are distinctively warlike, such a statement tends to carry more weight with us than if the distinction were made on the basis of blood type, hair color, or even the shape of the brain.

So if you are Asian, are you the product of superior genes for intelligence? If you are a black, Indian, or native Hawaiian American, are you the product of poorer ones? While I believe the evidence is clear for a strong inherited component to our individuality, there are few reasons for thinking that race has anything to do with it. Race, race differences, and understanding the real role of genetics in our lives have been much confused.

For some people, seriously considering genetic differences among races automatically leads to thinking about racial distinctions, or—even worse—to institutionalized discrimination, or—worse still—to savageness. For a long time now, for too long, genetic determinism has shaded into racial determinism, and the concept has been used to "justify" atrocities from the concentration camps to the killing fields to apartheid to ethnic cleansing. Not a happy lot. The serious question is how can we look at diversity and genetic inheritance with regard to racial difference without falling into any of these traps?

Since it has been so frequently studied, intelligence testing of racial differences can serve as a paradigm for looking at other parts of individuality. Paper-and-pencil tests are given to great numbers of people, and when people are classified by skin color, differences are scored. The evidence is straightforward, but it has been subject to different interpretations. Currently, on the biggest and most socially defining test, the IQ test, black, Indian, and native Hawaiian Americans score in the high eighties to the low nineties, while whites score about 100.

It would be amusing, were it not horrifying, to quote archaic postulations about what will happen if one group or another comes to power or if women get the vote, but consider what notable scientists have said about race and intelligence: Lewis Terman, the shaper of the Stanford-Binet standard IQ test, stated in 1919 that "high-grade moronity [was] very common among Spanish, Indian, and Mexican families . . . and also among Negroes."

Berkeley psychologist Arthur Jensen argued in 1969 that compensatory education programs that attempt to improve the intelligence of black children will fail because the difference in IQ is innate. Harvard's Richard Herrnstein, writing in 1977, thought that the United States would eventually develop into a "meritocracy" based on heredity.

> As the wealth and complexity of human society grow, there will be precipitated out of the mass of humanity a low-capacity [group of people] that . . . cannot compete for success and achievement and are more likely to be born to parents who have similarly failed. . . . The tendency to be unemployed may run in the genes of the family about as certainly as bad teeth do now.

Every ethnic group that has migrated to the United States has been the subject of these arguments. When the descendants of the people of the Renaissance first came to the United States, these Italian Americans were also considered to be of inferior intelligence.

In truth, the major differences among races are skin deep and superficial, like skin color, eye folds, and sweat glands. There is no evidence of difference in brain size, shape, organization, or structure among people of different races. But since skin is what we see, we tend to classify people in this way.

But even this classification into races is arbitrary and fuzzy. Only a small fraction of a group have the full set of racially associated traits. For instance, only 10 percent of a large sample of Swedish army officers were found to have blond hair and blue eyes, although these are traits we associate with the category of "a typical Swede."

In fact, such classifications are simply an abstraction when it comes to inheritance; a "race" never mothered or fathered anybody. *People get their genes from their parents, not from a racial group.* Analyses of genetic differences show that ethnic groups do not differ substantially in the type of genes found, but there are

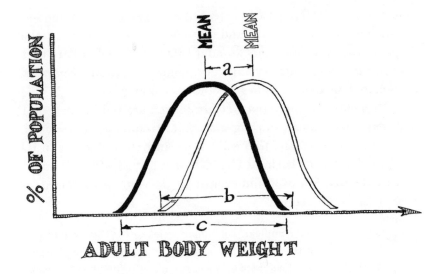

great differences among individuals within each ethnic group. The average genetic difference between two individual Italians or between two individual Malays is more than ten times greater than the average genetic difference between Italians and Malays.

Intelligence, Heredity, and IQ

Sandy Jackson is seven. She was just tested at an IQ of 70 and is "educable mentally retarded." She couldn't answer questions like "cup is to _____ as chair is to floor," since the answer is "saucer" and her family, a poor black one, doesn't have saucers. She wrote "table."

Her classification will set her along a caste line destined to keep her down.

The distribution of scores on the widely used Binet-type intelligence test has caused great controversy, since these IQ tests are used to classify children in schools. Those who score low—60 to 70, for example—may be placed in classes for the "educable mentally retarded." Sometimes this division is warranted and in the best interest of the child. There are some severely retarded or disturbed people who cannot function academically in a traditional public school classroom. However, much of the time, the standard tests discriminate against children whose backgrounds differ from the norm, and the norm is usually white, middle class, and male.

There *is* an inherited component to the elusive qualities we call intelligence, but it is the nature of that inheritance that is in question. Compare the relationship of IQ to genetic similarity. If IQ is inherited, then the more similar people's genetic structures are, the more similar their IQs should be. A large investigation at the University of Minnesota, headed by Thomas Bouchard, found that identical twins reared together correlate amazingly well (.86, close to the perfect correlation of 1.00); correlations of identical twins reared apart are less high but significant (.72); those of fraternal twins reared together are lower (.60); siblings reared together have a moderate association (.47); and siblings reared apart have a low association (.24). Many other genetic factors govern individual intelligence. While genetic structure seems to play only a moderate role in reading retardation, both spelling abilities and disabilities seem quite heritable.

In another major study at the University of Minnesota, Auke Tellegen and others administered the Multidimensional Personality Questionnaire to 217 identical and 114 fraternal reared-together adult twin pairs and 44 identical and 27 fraternal reared-apart adult twin pairs and then analyzed the results for genetic effects on such factors as interestedness, arousability, and lying. They found heritabilities ranging from .39 to .58, much higher than anyone would have previously believed. Even responsibility seems to have a genetic component.

Identical twins have an identical genetic makeup, and they also have the closest IQ resemblance. Next in similarity come fraternal twins and siblings; their similarity is less but still substantial. Parents and children also show a relationship, but as the genetic similarity decreases, so does the correspondence among IQs. Yet the environment also has an important effect. The IQs of genetically related children reared together are much more similar than those of genetically related children reared apart. The correlation between the IQ of foster parents and that of their foster children is about .30, a good indicator that the environment is important.

Still, the racial gap in IQs is consistent, and when we examine it, many new factors come out. The gap is similar to that between the entitled and powerless in many cultures. The disadvantaged, like the Sephardic Jews compared to the "favored" Ashkenazi Jews in Israel, score ten to fifteen points lower than the entitled do on IQ tests. But there is no such gap between Sephardic and Ashkenazi Jews in America.

If there's really something to racial effects, then it shouldn't matter whether one gets one's genes from one's father or mother. However, children of white mothers and black fathers have higher IQs than those of black mothers and white fathers, presumably because the white mothers talk to their children more than do the black mothers. Another study of the IQs of 129 children from interracial pairs showed the following: at the age of four, the relationship between the skin color of the mother and the IQ of the child is worth about six to seven IQ points, and this gap increases as experience diverges for the two groups.

John Ogbu, a Nigerian anthropologist, considers the critical factor to be the "lower-caste" worldview of certain groups. He suggests that the dispossessed see learning the main culture's ideas, which they do through school learning, as a form of disloyalty to their own culture. A study of two groups of equally bright black high school students, one doing well and one failing, bears out this idea. Those who were faring poorly felt that being studious was like "acting white." It's significant that the same gap in IQ and social success occurs wherever castelike divisions exist in society.

There are other groups in the United States who don't adopt this lower-caste mentality. Koreans, who are often the envy of blacks, and Chinese, who are the source of envy throughout the world, have most often immigrated to upgrade their status. Ogbu notes that they compare themselves with the poorer folk at home, not with the rich whites in the United States. Thus, even in menial jobs they tend to feel better off than before.

But the first American blacks were slaves, and American Indians and native Hawaiians are both conquered indigenous people. Andrew Hacker points out that the United States is the only nation that has specifically imported people for the purpose of slavery. The majority culture needed to justify their use of blacks as slaves, and the concept of inferiority was one good way. Thomas Jefferson, who kept slaves but who is often cited as having an "enlightened" attitude toward them, claimed only that black people should be given the chance to be free. He did not claim that they were equal in ability to whites.

Official segregation ended in the United States with *Brown vs. Board of Education,* and it is now the law that schools and jobs be as open to black people as to whites. But in practice, African Americans do not have the same environment as white Americans, and this has profound effects on them. Even today, as we shall see, the legacy of this oppression shunts many contemporary black people off the main line of their development. Many young African Americans grow up believing that they cannot attain the glittering prizes of this society. Many youngsters, stunted by a constant barrage of racial slurs, might believe that they could achieve the National Basketball Association's Most Valuable Player award but never a Nobel Prize or a senate seat, although these arenas are slowly changing. So why should impoverished black children take seriously the idea of making it in white society through the process of learning in school?

The derision goes on constantly. Think about these incidents, which I gathered in just a few days of browsing through a handful of newspapers. On the first day, a story described an ad that had appeared in a small newspaper just north of San Francisco. It included a mug shot of a fortysomething black man with a goatee. The text of the ad read: "WHAT WOULD YOU DO IF YOU SAW THIS MAN RIDING A BIKE THROUGH YOUR NEIGHBORHOOD?"

Antoine Bigirimana, the man who placed the ad, runs a software company in the town of Sonoma, California. But he hasn't been treated there like a typical computer entrepreneur. While riding to work, he had his bicycle confiscated, since the police thought they had good reason to believe it was stolen. One night, sitting in his own front yard, he was questioned for "lurking."

So he took the ad out, and it woke people up. Most people in the town don't own software companies; they also don't get stopped by the police. Sonoma is 97 percent white; a black is automatically thought of as an intruder.

Another local story appeared in the San Francisco *Chronicle.* Keith Debro, who works for United Airlines as a baggage handler, had filed a lawsuit against his employer for not removing the reprehensible racial graffiti that had been written inside the baggage holds of the planes that he has to unload. "I felt so awful, it's so vile. And I didn't feel like anyone should have to work in an environment like that. It was hateful to a lot of people, not just blacks. I began to hate my job," Debro said.

On Thursday, January 28, 1993, while changing channels, I noticed three young black men talking on a program I hadn't intended to watch. I stopped and listened. One young man said, "I'm not going to rob anybody; it's not in my nature. But it hurts if I get on the train and people think I'm going to rob them. And it happens every day."

The national edition of the New York *Times* carried a story about the new chancellor of a campus at the University of California. The man made a career move from his current position as the head of the National Science Foundation. He is identified as a "black physicist." Have you ever heard anybody described as a "white physicist"? "Isaac Newton, a white man, who discovered . . . "?

These examples were readily apparent in just a few days, with only a minor tour into the information easily available to me. It took almost no effort on my part. I haven't mentioned the daily experiences of people growing up in South Central Los Angeles or the blatantly shocking conditions that Jonathan Kozol describes in East Saint Louis, Illinois, in his *Savage Inequalities*. How many more millions of incidents exist? How many thousands don't make the papers? How many more airplanes, with rich and predominantly white people comfortably ensconced "upstairs," even now contain in their underbellies the scrawled remains of slavery?

I'm not saying that these examples are scientifically valid but that anybody can find such cases any day in our society. While we all know that skin color, because it is so apparent, makes it easy to prejudge someone, rarely has the unspoken been better said than by the Nobel laureate William Shockley:

> Nature has color-coded groups of individuals so that statistically reliable predictions of their adaptability to intellectually rewarding and effective lives can easily be made and profitably be used by the man in the street.
>
> PAUL EHRLICH AND SHIRLEY FELDMAN, *THE RACE BOMB: SKIN COLOR, PREJUDICE, AND INTELLIGENCE*

*I*Q tests measure adequately a child's ability to perform in school. These tests, however, are notoriously poor predictors of job success or of how well one will do financially as an adult, for example. That Japanese children score between four and eleven IQ points higher than Americans does not mean that the Japanese are that much "smarter" than Americans but reflects their being raised with extreme parental and social pressure, working very long hours, and taking no vacations.

Head Start and similar programs that enrich the child's environment are known to produce large IQ gains—from five to twenty-five points—in a single generation. Some of this effect may result simply from a person coming in to talk to the child for a few extra hours per day. Consider the IQ changes of castelike minorities who emigrate. When they settle in a place free from discrimination, their children's IQ scores and school performance match those of other children.

These are some of the social factors that influence differences in IQ; now let's consider some physical components of the differences. The average difference in early environment for blacks and whites in the United States, even today, is so great—in nutrition, leading to differences in birth weight, in exposure to pollution and toxins, in use of drugs—that these alone could well account for any test differences.

A small head size for age and sex predicts mental retardation. Except in cases of major disorders such as hydrocephalus or other cranial pathology, head size reflects the growth of the brain. Head circumference reaches about 96 percent of adult size at age ten. Many investigations throughout the world have found that malnutrition, especially in a child's early years, reduces the normal rate of head growth. This insufficient growth alone accounts for five to six points of the IQ differences found between black and white communities.

In the study cited earlier on the impact of low birth weight, all LBW children were shorter and had smaller heads than normal-birth-weight children. They also had a later onset of puberty. Children born at 2,000 grams did less well than those born at 2,500. The least impairment occurred among LBW children of nonmanual workers. A British study surveying verbal reasoning scores of fifty thousand children found a continuous increase in a child's score with higher birth weight and with a rise in social status (as defined by the father's job).

Do those in different skin-color groups begin life equally well nourished and at equal birth weights? A major survey of birth weights in the United States showed the following: whites have a mean birth weight of 3,286 grams; blacks have a mean birth weight of 3,069. Were we to institute a real "affirmative action" that improved nutrition and equalized birth weights, the best assumption is that there would be an IQ gain of about five points for African American children.

Even vitamin C levels have effects. One study focused on children in the fourth, fifth, and sixth grades. Children with high ascorbic acid levels (more than 1.1 milligram of ascorbic acid per 100 milliliters (mg./ml.) of blood plasma) were separated statistically from those with low ascorbic acid (0.6 milligrams per 100 milliliters) and studied for IQ. The mean IQ for children with higher levels of ascorbic acid was 113; for those with lower levels, it was 110. When ascorbic acid was given as a supplement, the mean IQ of the group with lower ascorbic acid moved up to 113.

A major nutrition survey found median ascorbic acid levels for blacks in high-income states like Washington as 0.95 mg./ml. of vitamin C and in low-income states like Alabama as 0.45 mg./ml. If we were to offer ascorbic acid supplementation to the population, there would be a three-point rise in IQ scores for African Americans in low-income states.

With all these shackles (and we don't even have a good estimate on the increased lead and groundwater pollution in black areas compared with those of whites, for instance), the case for any genetic "racial" difference affecting IQ becomes difficult if not impossible to contemplate. And it isn't as if the vestiges of racism have been eliminated by the civil rights era in the United States, either. It's part of the ongoing fabric of our life.

There are many abstractions that confuse us regarding individuality. That you come from a specific ethnic group is inevitable, but that you carry the supposed characteristics of that group is not. Recall that all of us learn languages, but our ability to learn Sanskrit or Japanese with the same ease as in youth disappears forever after we learn the first language. Experience, not race, makes this difference. That's my personal view. It is simply because race is such a visible marker of difference that we are often confused by it.

However, if we are to make changes in society, we need to help mothers early on, improving maternal nutrition and thereby infant birth weight, and we need to talk more to our children and to educate them. All these things might go a long way toward reducing social inequality and eventually eroding simplistic stereotypes. But one's skin color is no key at all to the kind of person you are. Skin color is skin deep and means little or nothing more. People get their genes from their families, not from a racial group. There is more to discover in what goes on in the family than in an abstraction like "race."

Chapter 11

Why Are Children in the Same Family So Dissimilar?

I don't usually follow the New York Yankees, having left their domain twenty-five years ago; besides, since I grew up in Brooklyn, I was a Dodger fan anyway. However, a story in the March 2, 1992, sports pages of the New York *Times* caught my eye. The article concerns two brothers who now play for the Yankees. They grew up in San Cristobal in the Dominican Republic, with no baseball gear, in dusty streets. They were raised in a tiny house. Poor? Melido Perez says, "Yeah, big time."

They both now play professional baseball. Pascual Perez is the cutup; he occasionally wears wild jumpsuits, plays pranks, and is very gregarious. Melido keeps to himself, is friendly but never intrudes on anyone else. He wears regular sports shirts and jeans and does not flash the Fort Knox cache of gold jewelry that his brother wears. It is difficult to believe, the article implies, that they could come from the same family.

In Simone de Beauvoir's report in her autobiography of the differences between her sister and herself, the author hints at one possible source of those differences—birth order—which we will discuss in this chapter:

> I had been a new experience for my parents; my sister found it much more difficult to surprise and astonish them; I had never been compared with anyone else: she was always being compared with me. . . . In the photographs that were taken of me at two and a half I have a determined and self-confident expression; hers at the same age show a timid frightened look.
>
> QUOTED IN DUNN AND PLOMIN, *SEPARATE LIVES*

Elements vary between siblings

We tend to think that children in the same family will grow up to be more similar than unrelated people. This is a fundamental part of our lore: brothers who are alike in their disdain for convention or sisters who both take up the law. However, comprehensive studies in Sweden, Great Britain, the United States, Finland, and other countries show that a shared family environment does not affect children's personalities at all! This is because, even within a family, each child grows up in a thoroughly different world from the others.

Although siblings share many genes, other factors, including birth order, make children live in distinct worlds and develop quite differently even in the same home. The research leads to a radical conclusion: *families do not make us similar to our siblings; they make us different*. Genetics accounts for similarities among children in the same families, but it is family experiences that make them different. Most parents, for instance, treat girls differently from boys and firstborns differently from those born later.

For example, two sisters were at a dinner party when the conversation turned to upbringing. The elder sister started to say that her parents had been very strict and that she had been rather frightened of them. Her sister, younger by two years, interrupted in amazement. "What are you talking about?" she said. "Our parents were very lenient. I remember being allowed to stay out late and to do all sorts of things. How could you call them strict?"

Both were accurate: one sister had received different treatment from the other. The first child had borne the brunt of parental anxiety all through her childhood and was stopped from doing things that might possibly be dangerous or unsuitable. But by the time the younger one was growing up, the parents had learned to relax a bit, since the first daughter hadn't gotten into

We combine an inheritance from our parents

trouble, and they were much more likely to let the second daughter have her head.

We often take for granted that children in a family have had the same sorts of experiences and that these will make them very similar: that an authoritarian father is authoritarian with all his children; that a kindly parent is perceived as kindly by all the offspring. But this is simply not the case.

Although certain personality traits do run in families, siblings are far more different than they are alike. When they are tested, their scores are as different as those of unrelated people brought up separately. Most of us have siblings; presumably, therefore, most of us know how different we are from them. Yet we're usually amazed to find out that someone who is, say, shy and retiring and someone who is outgoing and overbearing are actually brothers or sisters.

It isn't amazing. Long-term studies find that only certain beliefs—for instance, about religion, politics, or attitudes about males and females—are influenced by coming from the same family. How can this be?

Siblings have only a fifty-fifty chance of inheriting the same gene from their parents. And since behavior is not influenced by any one major gene but by many, the likelihood of siblings being genetically identical in the areas of behavior and personality is quite remote. Certainly genetics does account for some of the differences between siblings. However, since different gene structures explain only part of siblings' behavior and personality differences, the rest of the explanation is likely to be found among environmental influences. Twin and adoption studies bear this out.

Yet isn't it strange that environment accounts for so much *difference* between siblings when so much of their environment is shared—home, family, rituals, food, and so on? Once again, twin and adoption studies show that whatever experiences *are* shared by siblings do not have a bearing on personality development; otherwise, siblings would be much more similar than nonsiblings— and they are not.

Consider the incidence of schizophrenia. If identical twins are different in many ways, the reason must be nongenetic, as they share all their genes. Identical twins are less than 50 percent similar for schizophrenia, so if one has it and the other doesn't, the reason must lie in some environmental impact that has not been shared by both.

So if siblings are so different and if most of their differences are accounted for by environment, they must share far less of their environment than we have until now imagined. In other words, they must be treated differently or perceive themselves as being treated differently, thus giving rise to a completely different environmental experience.

The Influence of Birth Order on Individuality

The idea that birth order can foretell personality originated with Alfred Adler, an Austrian physician born in 1870. His own early background may have guided his theory. The second child among five siblings, he was a delicate boy very aware of his inferiority to his older, strong, and vigorously healthy brother (in fact, Adler went on to invent the term *inferiority complex*). Even as an accomplished older man, Adler continued to believe—and to deplore the thought—that he failed to rival his brother.

As a physician, Adler developed an interest in the environmental effects on physical and psychological health. Erudite and outspoken, he was discovered by Freud in 1902, who invited Adler to be part of his elite group of colleagues. However, the friendship faltered ten years later when Freud began quarreling with and suppressing the gifted Adler. Freud was thirteen years Adler's senior and, not surprisingly, sought authority in their relationship. (Freud is supposed to have once said to a friend, "I am by temperament nothing but a conquistador.") Adler, of the same birth position, felt stifled and he departed.

Frank Sulloway found that later-born scientists of eminence compared to firstborns were more likely to promote revolutionary ideas. Copernicus, Freud, and Darwin were all later-borns. Of eight hundred eminent scientists who either supported or opposed major revolutionary ideas, 60 percent of the later-borns were in favor of the creative hypothesis, compared to support from only about 40 percent of the firstborns. More scientists who opposed the novel idea were firstborns.

In a large 1950s study, two-thirds of the 360 five- and six-year-olds who were asked how their parents treated them and their siblings said that either they or their sibling was favored by their mother. In contrast to Simone de Beauvoir's account, in this study it was usually the firstborn who felt hard done by. More recent studies confirm that siblings usually perceive a difference in the way they are treated by their parents.

Even very young children react to a newborn. In a study by Judy Dunn and her colleagues at Cambridge University in Great Britain, in the months after the birth of a second baby, the first child interrupted three out of four exchanges between mother and baby, usually to protest or to demand the same treatment. Often the older child will carry out whatever action of the baby has pleased the mother or excited attention, whether the action is clever or naughty. Sometimes the older child will just try to join in or else will try to disrupt play between mother and baby. Sometimes he or she will just cry with the distress of it all.

Firstborns are very much aware of the difference in tone that their mothers use when talking to them rather than to their sibling. If the mother has just turned from scolding the older child for behaving in an annoying way to respond warmly and affectionately to the gurgles of the baby, it's no surprise that the children experience the difference. Such partiality is no doubt noted at once and may well play a part in developmental differences between the siblings.

It isn't just firstborns who are aware in this way, although, of course, their jealousy is particularly explicable. Secondborn children, too, are very aware of what is going on between mothers and firstborns and particularly join in disputes, usually to support the mother against the sibling. They are especially keen, too, to

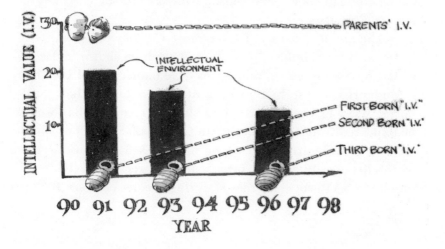

turn the attention back to themselves when the mother and elder child are talking or playing together.

For millennia, the firstborn (male, at least) has been regarded as the heir, the favored one, the one destined to assume family leadership upon the death of the father. Recent evidence somewhat surprisingly confirms that firstborns are better leaders but also shows that later birth has its advantages, too.

Firstborns have higher IQ. A child's intellectual development is related to the intellectual abilities of the people in his or her immediate environment, namely the family. The fewer the children in that world, the higher, on average, the intellectual level. To determine the intellectual level of the family environment, Robert Zajonc used a mathematical formula in which he assigned people "intelligence values" proportional to their ages, with a maximum of thirty. Thus, the first child is born into an environment of thirty for the first parent plus thirty for the second plus zero for the baby, divided by three for an average of twenty.

If the next child is born when the first child has an intellectual level of four, then the intellectual value of his environment is, similarly

$$\frac{30 + 30 + 4 + 0}{4} = 16$$

The first child is born into an environment with the highest possible intellectual value for that family. Each new child is born into a successively lower one. In addition, most older children teach their younger siblings in many ways—through games, behavior, and language—and this may increase the older child's intellectual abilities.

The average scores of the almost 800,000 participants in National Merit Scholarship programs have been shown to decline as family size increases. Firstborns have higher verbal IQs than secondborns, and secondborns, in turn, score higher than thirdborns. Many more eminent scientists are firstborns than would be expected from their number in the population. Thus, birth order and family size have a lasting effect, at least on those aspects of intelligence measured by scientific careers and IQ tests. Similarly, SAT scores decreased during the period from 1963 to

1980 when there were increases in family size. The trend reversed itself in 1980 when family size declined.

Firstborns tend to be more cautious, nervous, and anxious than those born later. Firstborns and those born later are treated differently by their parents, and these effects continue into later life. Generally, mothers pay more attention to their firstborns. They are more strict with and protective of their firstborns, preventing them from doing things for fear of harm. At just less than four years of age, firstborns obey their parents more than do those born later. Later in life, firstborns seem to be more inhibited than those born later.

Firstborns are also more conformist, less likely to express antisocial sentiments. They remain a little more physically fearful as well, generally preferring safer sports, such as swimming, to gymnastics or skiing. They are also usually more nervous. During a power blackout in New York City, people were asked, "How nervous and uneasy were you during the experience?" Firstborns were more anxious and distressed.

Later-borns, being less anxious and inhibited, are more likely to be socially popular, but they are also more likely to harbor doubts about themselves. Because they do not have as much of their parents' attention as they want, they may feel that others do not like them very much.

The Child in the Family

The presence of siblings also changes the time it takes to learn social relationships. Normally children do not learn about social relationships with their friends until they are seven or eight years old, but within families, they start much sooner. In one study, a rather withdrawn two-and-a-half-year-old boy sadly responded to his mother's proud description of his outgoing little sister as a determined little devil by saying, "I'm not a determined little devil." Already he knew how different he was from her and how her behavior (but possibly not his) incited pride in his mother.

Parents certainly treat their children differently. William James, the eminent psychologist, and his younger brother, the novelist Henry, are further examples of the way in which siblings are treated differently. Their mother (according to Henry's biographer Leon Edel) treated William as self-absorbed and a hypochondriac whenever he claimed to be ill as an adult, while she made a great fuss over any illness of Henry's.

You might think that most parents would not be able to admit to differences in the way they treat their children because we believe that we ought to treat all our children the same. However, in separate studies carried out on mothers in Colorado and mothers in Cambridge, only a third said that they felt the same amount of affection for both children or that they gave equal attention to both. Only 12 percent of both groups thought that they dished out discipline equally. Also, in both studies, more mothers favored the younger of the siblings.

One other finding from the Colorado studies goes a long way toward explaining why most siblings develop so differently. Mothers react to different children similarly at each age. That is, when each child was one year old, he or she was treated with a great deal of affection, but when each child was two, the mother was somewhat less openly affectionate. So the mothers were consistent in how they treated all children of a certain age. However, the children themselves would not be able to recognize this; a two-year-old would simply be acutely aware that he or she was receiving less affection than the baby.

The researchers suggest, "Seeing your mother's evident affection for your sibling may override any amount of affection you in fact receive." This view is contrary to the conventional one, in which it is believed that how a parent relates directly to a child is what affects development. When we realize that the child is aware not only of how he or she is treated but also of how any siblings are treated, the emphasis shifts from the child-parent interaction alone to the child's position as family member.

How a child relates to others may be linked to how that child has experienced being loved within the family. *Experienced* is the operative word here. Even if the parents were equally loving to all the children, if a child felt a difference for whatever reason, that difference will affect the way that child feels about himself or herself and others. As Charles Dickens wrote in *Great Expectations*, "In the little world in which children have their existence, there is nothing so finely perceived, and so finely felt, as injustice."

Dickens himself was obliged to go to work in a factory at the age of twelve, while his sister Fanny won a scholarship to the Royal Academy of Music. He felt terribly humiliated and deprived not to have the chance to shine as Fanny had done and prayed each night to be lifted out of the neglect he felt he suffered.

In one national study, the sibling who had been closest to the mother was more involved in family decision making, was the recipient of higher expectations, and was the better adjusted psychologically. Conversely, according to the Colorado study, children who felt that they were disciplined more by their mothers and received less affection were more likely to be anxious or depressed. Getting less favorable treatment from the mother can also encourage disobedient, argumentative, hyperactive, and antisocial behavior.

It isn't so much that a child's innate nature causes parents to treat him or her differently from other siblings; rather, it is the differences in the way children are treated by their parents that create the differences in the children's adjustment. Children's sense of self-worth is very much related to how they perceived they were treated by their parents, as well as to their own personality differences. This is important, because poor self-worth can lead to difficulty in relationships with others.

Differences in the way children treat each other could also be an important source of the differences between siblings' personalities not always by any means explained by birth order or gender. In about a fifth of all interactions between siblings, they are not mutually friendly or mutually hostile.

The greater the difference between the affection shown by the older child to the younger and that shown by the younger to the older, the more likely the older child is to be depressive and antisocial. And the bigger the difference between hostility doled out by the elder and hostility received by him or her, the greater the likelihood of lower self-esteem. A child is aware of everything about his or her siblings—how they act, what motivates them, what hurts or pleases them, how successful and popular they are. Siblings constantly make comparisons that have a significant impact on each one's self-evaluation.

Inevitably, as children grow, they start to have a life outside of their family. They go to school, they take up hobbies according to their interests and talents, they make different friends, and eventually, they go on to college or start work. When the eldest child moves away from the family, the relationship between him or her and a younger sibling can begin to lack "mutuality." Suddenly, the older child is caught up in an exciting new existence from which the younger is excluded, and their intense closeness lessens.

Later Childhood

*I*t isn't only what happens in our early formative years that has an impact on who and what we become. On the contrary, what happens in later childhood, in teenage years, and well into adulthood can change or add to the effects of those early years.

Chance events, such as the death of a parent, can have very different effects on different children, particularly if one or the other was significantly closer to the parent who died. Other chance events may happen to one sibling and not another; being mauled by a dog or being sexually molested by a trusted uncle, for example, can have a dramatic impact on the child well into adulthood. All of these circumstances help to account for differences among siblings.

Also crucial might be shared life events that have different effects on different members of the family. Moving to another state, for instance, might have no major impact on a preschool child but have quite a devastating one on an older sibling who must lose friends and change schools. The Cambridge study reveals several such examples. One family, for instance, moved away when the elder girl was seven and the brother was three. The latter adapted easily, as his parents and sister were still the mainstay of his life. The girl had an unhappy time, trying to settle into a school where there was an in-group of girls from whom she was excluded. She reacted badly and as a consequence received an unkind label that dogged her for several years.

The Impact of Divorce on Children's Development

*O*ne important determination of the child's development is whether the parents stay together. Currently, the rate of divorce is at an all-time high. In 1964, there was one divorce for every four marriages, but by the nineties there was more than one divorce for every two marriages. Approximately one-half of all children growing up in the 1980s experienced the separation or divorce of their parents.

Not surprisingly, childless couples are most likely to divorce, and the more children a couple has, the more stable is their marriage. But surprisingly, the sex of the children also seems to be related to how stable the marriage is. Couples who have only daughters are the most likely to divorce, while couples who have only sons are the least likely.

It has been assumed that divorce is better for children than living in a family environment characterized by strife and bitterness. Most parents who divorce do describe themselves as feeling freer and better off. However, a large study by Judy Wallerstein in San Francisco finds surprisingly negative effects of divorce. The children themselves do not feel happier, in part because they did not experience the same conflict that their parents went through. Now they have to deal with one parent, who gives them less attention and is more involved in rebuilding a new life.

Eighteen months after the breakup, two-thirds of the children of divorce do not see their families as better off than before the divorce. More children accept the divorce with time, especially the adolescents and those who have maintained a good relationship with both parents. Five years later, however, 56 percent still do not feel their family life is better.

Nearly all children show some degree of distress at the news of parental separation, although it may not be initially apparent. Children feel frightened and more vulnerable; they may feel an enormous sense of loss and may worry about the emotional state of their parents, about who will feed them, and about where they will live. They also worry about their own relationship with their parents—if their parents could stop loving each other, why not them, too? Will their father prefer his new girlfriend, or maybe his stepchildren, to them? The children and adolescents may feel angry, rejected, and torn by conflicting loyalties to both parents.

Most of all, the children feel lonely. One parent, generally the father, has left the household, and the mother is now less available to them, due to her own anxiety and, often, to the need to work full time.

How children respond to the divorce depends greatly on their age and how the parents handle the divorce. Preschool children most often react with fear, guilt, bewilderment, and regression. Few children of this age are prepared for such a separation, and they awake one morning stunned to find a parent gone. This stimulates fear of abandonment by both parents and macabre fantasies to explain the loss.

On the other hand, children from six to eight years old respond mostly with grief. They may cry a great deal and express intense yearning for the departed parent. Boys may express considerable anger at the mother for either causing the divorce or driving the father away.

Children nine to twelve years of age are better able to handle grief, but they also express intense anger at their parents. They are the most likely to become involved in the battles between their parents, often taking sides with one against the other, which is particularly detrimental to a smooth adjustment to post-divorce life.

Adolescents with a relatively separate identity and the support coming from many friendships tend to cope well, maturing even more rapidly as a result of this experience. Others, however, especially those with low self-esteem, tend to regress or "act out" through sexual promiscuity, drugs, or alcohol.

Continued conflict between the parents after the divorce can have a devastating impact on the children. The children who do best are those who have easy access to the separated parent (generally the father), who maintain a good relationship with him or her, and whose custodial parent (generally the mother) is able to regain her or his own internal equilibrium, providing a reasonably well-organized and secure household and being emotionally available to the children.

There are other effects of divorce, including poverty, especially for the mother, and other later events that might seem surprising: girls who are quite young when their parents divorce, for example, come into sexual maturity six months earlier, have their own children earlier, and separate from their partners earlier than children whose parents stay together. Boys from families where the father is absent because of divorce often behave in an exaggeratedly macho way, and girls from similar homes are more promiscuous during their teenage years. Yet this pattern isn't repeated for boys or girls reared by mothers whose husbands have died. Why?

I am going to consider this aspect, controversial as it is, because it is related to the major question of how our experiences in early life select from the newborn's innate faculties and thus help adjust the self to the locale in which it grows up. It also connects this discussion of family and early experience with the important question of how our sexuality and sexual style relate to the self.

To develop my argument, I want to consider an evolutionary explanation for why animals and human beings behave in different ways in different environments. Since the central biological focus of life is to ensure successful reproduction, behaviors that lead to increases in surviving offspring get "selected" over time. Each organism has to determine how best to go about reproducing in its environment. Human beings, who grow up in very varying circumstances throughout the world, do not have a fixed strategy, but "select" some of their many innate faculties to use them in the environment in which they are born. Biologists use the terms *r-selection* and **K-selection** to describe the different mating strategies of different species. The r-selected organisms, like insects and fish, have developed in unstable environments where a lot of their number are quite likely to be wiped out at any time. These organisms become sexually active early, reproduce quickly and copiously, leave their young to take care of themselves quite early, and die off sooner.

K-selected organisms, on the other hand, live in much better environmental conditions. They become sexually mature much later, have fewer young (usually single offspring rather than large litters), and take care of their young for years rather than weeks. Mammals are much more K-selected than birds or insects. But mammals, too, can be divided into r and K: gerbils are more r-selected, for instance, while elephants more K-selected. Humans are the most K-selected of all mammals.

Still, even among humans there are variations, as the statistics on the sexuality of children of divorced parents show. In some groups, the norm is for two-parent upbringing and strict control of adolescents' burgeoning sexuality; in others, the parents are not strongly bonded, it isn't expected

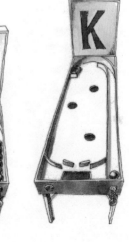

that the father will stay around, and the sexual codes that the children learn are far less strict, so they become sexually active earlier. The children may not be left to fend entirely for themselves, but they may instead be looked after mostly by neighbors or other caregivers or relatives.

But what is the logic behind the different sexual behaviors of children who grow up in two-parent households versus those who grow up in single-parent households? If we think about these behaviors in evolutionary terms, we begin to see that each set is equally "right" for the children's circumstances.

The world of the family gives the developing child a "snapshot" of the likely environment in which he or she will grow up. Thus, we learn one or a few of the thousands of languages, a style of eating and relating, whether war is continuous or we're at peace, and thousands of other ways in which the world works. In the first five to seven years of their lives, children also develop attitudes that direct their later sexual and reproductive behavior.

Early experiences with their primary caregivers have a strong effect on how children develop emotionally. It would make sense for those who "learn" from their parents or caregivers that relationships last and can be trusted to follow a K-selected reproductive strategy. Similarly, it makes sense for those who were neglected and felt insecure to go for r-selected ones, because in their world relationships are short term and partners cannot be relied on for long.

Patricia Draper and Henry Harpending find that children whose fathers were absent are sexually active earlier, and this increases their reproductive potential in a chancy environment. It makes reproductive sense for people who grow up in an unstable environment—one with violence, transient sexual encounters, and the like—to have children as early as possible and with different partners. As they are not good at relationships, they would be likely to lose out if they waited for Mr. or Ms. Right before having children. In contrast, teenagers from homes with two parents tend to delay sexual activity and be interested in forming a lasting relationship.

Chance events such as the death of a parent could have very different effects on different children, if one or the other was significantly closer to the parent who died. Or, as mentioned earlier, other chance events may happen to one sibling and not another.[1]

We've covered a lot of ground about the family, but I want to reiterate the main point here: we misinterpret the family when we assume that it is a significant source of similarity in individuals. "Coming from a dysfunctional family" is a shibboleth these days. And from the beginning of psychoanalysis, this unit has been thought of as the root of individual differences. It isn't, as individuals in the same family are no more alike than most unrelated strangers on almost all measures. Psychologist Hans Eysenck said it well:

> Traditional theories from Freud onwards concerning the major influence on personality of the family (and associated influences such as socioeconomic status and education) now appear to be wrong. This result alone necessitates a revolution in current thinking about the development of personality.

As we've seen, different sexual strategies are brought about in some children by the early world in which they live. But how different are the general sexual strategies of the two sexes themselves? And how different in mind are the sexes? We will take up these questions in the next chapter.

---

1. Of course, other factors may also weigh heavily—for instance, absent-father homes are also likely to be low-income homes. But this doesn't explain the differences between families where the parents are divorced and those in which the father has died.

Chapter 12

Differences in Body

Sex Matters

"*B*iology is destiny," wrote Freud, spearheading a view that women and men undergo different kinds of development. In reaction, some people are now determined to blur any sex differences. Are these differences like those of race, where they are mostly the result of social status and other environmental factors? Or are they more like the differences between two species, where certain abilities are biologically determined? Or are they a little of both? While skin color is trivial in determining the self, sex does matter; it is an important biological fact.[1] However, sex doesn't matter in the way in which we conduct our business or other professional life, and it matters little in the way we speak and relate. *Sex differences matter most in matters sexual.* As we consider areas further and further away from sexuality itself, sex differences matter less and less. Thus, males and females may well differ in their sexual strategies, such as mate selection. They may even have differences in spatial perception and in certain components of verbal and mathematical ability, but

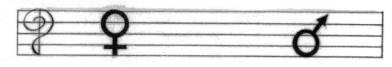

these are very small indeed. In fact, if we look to sex as a basis for differences in abilities in mathematics, music, writing, and the like, we are probably looking in the wrong place. The right place is the way in which each of us learns to act in the world.

---

1. We need to distinguish between the terms *sex* and *gender,* since many confuse the two. Sex is a matter of biology. Whether you're a female or a male is determined at conception. However, how a female and how a male are "supposed" to act within a society is a gender issue; it is not a biological but a social phenomenon. That more males like sports and more females like dance relates to gender, not to sex.

PREGNANCY

PREFERENCE FOR POWERFUL MATE

ANXIETY & DEPRESSION

THINKING OF SYNONYMS

EMPATHY

MATH CALCULATION

INTELLIGENCE

WORK ETHIC

TECHNICAL COMPETENCE

WRITING ABILITY

SUPERVISORY CAPACITY

READING

LEADERSHIP

MATH VISIO-SPATIAL

AGGRESSION

SPATIAL LOCATION

MUSCLE MASS

SEXUAL JEALOUSY-ATTITUDE TOWARDS INFIDELITY

SPERM PRODUCTION

Females and males differ on few dimensions

Remember how much difference learning a language makes: it sets us along a developmental course from which we can never emerge.

In our society, people tend to believe that men are more likely to be independent, competitive, competent, and task-oriented than women. Mathematics, engineering, and science, in general, are fields in which males rather than females are expected to excel. Little surprise, then, that males comprise about 84 percent of the United States' physicians, although the number of female M.D.s is now rapidly rising: the number of women physicians in this country increased 400 percent between 1970 and 1989.

In full-time jobs, women earn two-thirds as much as men. Female corporate vice-presidents earn 42 percent less than men in comparable positions. Can these differences in earnings be justified by differences in the competence of men and women? To be perfectly clear, the answer is NO.

But this is not to suggest that men and women are the same: there are many physical differences between the sexes. The most notable are in the reproductive systems, body size and weight, and muscle mass. Males on the average are more physically active at an earlier age than are females and are characteristically superior to females in tasks that require gross motor control and spatial abilities. In this chapter, we will first take a look at these actual differences between men and women, and then we will analyze what these differences mean and how much they matter.

Reproduction and Sexuality

Many differences between women and men are trivial. Reproductive differences certainly are not. The ability to bear children as well as the accompanying physiological effort and responsibility can make the life of a woman very different from that of a man. In all probability, this difference is the root of all the socially emphasized divisions between the roles and status of men and women. Now, thanks to contraception, women are freer to choose what they would like to be and how to conduct their lives.

Sex differences matter most in sexual matters since sexual behavior is essential to the survival of any species. Thus, anything that improves one's ability to reproduce is likely to be passed on to one's progeny. Behavior that impedes reproduction (such as not mating often enough or well enough or not investing properly in one's offspring) will result in the eventual dwindling of the line that carries the genes for this poor reproductive behavior.

Recall our discussion in the previous chapter of r-selection and K-selection mating strategies. The simplest way to think about "reproductive fitness" is to realize that (1) whichever genes are copied the most will predominate over the others and (2) the genes that carry instructions for their organisms to produce the most reproductively successful copies will win.

In most animals, the sexes are quite different in physical form and reproductive behavior. In lions, for instance, one dominant male mates with several females, all of whom live in a group. The male has multiple mates, while the females share a single one. Have humans, in this case, transcended the automatic inborn controls that drive lower animal behavior by restricting our mating? We might need to know more about our evolutionary history in order to say.

Approaching sexuality in evolutionary terms can tell us a lot about the way we currently go about our reproductive behavior. Since reproduction is the part of life most central for evolution, it is most susceptible to selection by evolution. For instance, a baby is a major biological event in a woman's body and life. Even if she doesn't breast-feed the baby, she carries it for nine months. Thus, human females are capable of producing only a few offspring in their lives. For a woman to have twenty babies in a lifetime would be remarkable indeed, while the *Guinness Book of World Records* lists the maximum number fathered by one man at over three thousand. A woman has at the most four hundred or so viable eggs and would need over three hundred years to bring them all to term, even if each egg was fertilized the very day of each birth.

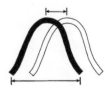

Human males, on the other hand, produce many millions of sperm per ejaculation and are capable of replicating their genes by conceiving new offspring daily or even more often. Strictly for the purpose of reproduction, the male can produce the most genetic copies of himself by engaging in reproductive behaviors as frequently as possible—and with as many different mates as possible. And statistically it is true that at all ages males have more sexual episodes per week than do females. These may be opposite-sex, same-sex, or same-person activities.[2]

For a woman to have the greatest opportunity to replicate her genes in new organisms that live long enough to copy them again (the everyday name for this is "babies"), she is better off carefully choosing mates who will give her viable children and who, ideally, will help her to raise them. Human fathers stay with their offspring and care for them much more than do other primates, and it is thought by many evolutionary biologists that repeated sexual activity between mates cements this bond. So even when a couple's physical sex act isn't aimed at reproduction, it may contribute to the survival of their genes in the children already born.

From an evolutionary perspective, then, we can make predictions about several important areas in which human male and female mate preferences may be affected by the differences in how men and women produce offspring. Women would be wise, for instance, to choose mates who will invest their resources, such as food, protection, child care, and social status, in the success of their children.

Psychologist David Buss suggests that this criterion for males could be perceived as "earning capacity" and ambition or industriousness. He notes that females of many nonhuman species mate "preferentially with males bearing greater gifts, holding better territories, or displaying higher rank." These advantages could also serve as indicators of greater genetic viability, so that the

---

2. This finding, controversial as it is, is consistent and is based on large group averages throughout all societies throughout the world. But as with any group difference, it doesn't hold for everybody. Some women certainly prefer sex more often than do some men, and some women have a "multiple-partner" sexual preference while some men have a monogamous preference. It is the case that on average, there are somewhat more "multiple-preference" men in the world population than there are women.

"top" males would be more likely to produce strong, dominant off-spring who are likely themselves to reproduce.

Human males, according to evolutionary principles, should have two overriding concerns with respect to their mates. The female mates should be fertile—that is, likely to bear children. Women's fertility peaks in their early twenties and declines over the next two decades, terminating at middle age. Men should be primed to prefer women of that age as partners.

Second, if a male is to invest his resources in a female and her children, he needs to be sure that he is fostering his own genes, not those of other men. Male sexual jealousy, responsible for close to a quarter of homicides, clearly could be driven by this biological "imperative," as could the social tradition of establishing a high value on female "chastity," meaning in this context the reluctance of a female to seek many mates.

The question of sexual fidelity is difficult to identify with specific character traits or physical features. One study tried to analyze it in terms of behavior. In this study of American college undergraduates, student couples watched scenes of their boyfriends or girlfriends interacting suggestively with persons of the opposite sex and then answered questions about their feelings. The men tended to express unpleasant fantasies about their girlfriends being sexually involved with the other men, while the women tended to fear loss of time and attention from their boyfriends due to their interest in the other women.

Perhaps because of the difficulty of determining paternity, jealousy is experienced differently between the sexes. Think about this question:

> What would upset or distress you more: (a) imagining your mate having sexual intercourse with someone else or (b) imagining your mate forming a deep emotional attachment to someone else?

Eighty-five percent of the women found the second choice more disturbing, while only 40 percent of the men did. Looked at another way, 60 percent of the men and only 15 percent of the women, one-fourth as many, found sexual infidelity more disturbing. And their bodily reactions confirmed these findings, as men showed a larger stress reaction (increased heart rate, skin conductance, and frowning) to the imagined infidelity than to the emotional disloyalty, while women showed the reverse.

One good way to determine whether mate preferences are inherently different between the sexes is to investigate these preferences in diverse cultures. David Buss surveyed thirty-seven cultures from all over the world and found a remarkable consistency in mating choices. Being a "good financial prospect" was rated as an important characteristic in a mate by females more often than by males in all of the cultures surveyed.

"Ambitiousness and industriousness" received high ratings as a desirable mate trait from both sexes in all cultures, but females valued it more than males in the vast majority of cultures. And in all the cultures, men preferred mates younger than themselves by an average of three to four years. Males expressed a desire for marriage at an average age of twenty-eight years, and the average age of their ideal female mate was twenty-four years old, about the age of peak fertility. (There *is* an identifiable group of males who do consistently prefer older women. These are the males who are sixteen to nineteen years old, and these "older women" are, of course, about twenty-two to twenty-four—again, at their reproductive peak.)

Women universally indicated a preference for older mates. Although this finding had not been a prediction of the theory, it could be further evidence of the female desire to have mates who are better providers, for most men acquire more resources with age.

Perhaps the most controversial idea is that men might prize beauty in women more highly than the reverse. Buss's study bore out this notion as well; in all thirty-seven cultures, men cared more about a mate's physical appearance than did women. (See Notes for Chaper Twelve, page 219.)

The findings for chastity were not as clear-cut as the others. In more than half of the cultures, the men were more interested in having mates without previous sexual experience than the women were. However, in many of the cultures, there was no difference between the sexes on this preference. If this is an area of human life affected by genetic pressures, it is also strongly influenced by the cultural environment.

While we don't know how genes can regulate mate preferences, it is clear that, with conscious effort, human beings can override preferences that carry us in directions against our personal, social, or cultural ideals. The same is true in other areas of life. For example, in the environment in which our ancestors evolved, discovering a cache of ready calories was rare; more of our forebears survived who ate a diet that was heavy on the fats and sugars in order to help ensure their day-to-day survival. Today, however, many people learn to give up sweets and fatty foods, choosing to eat lower-calorie vegetables and such, because food is plentiful for most and because the current myth is that long-term health is better served by a low-calorie, low-fat diet.

In a similar way, our ability to overrule genetics can serve us well in those areas where the inherited tendencies for male and female mate selection may cause social discord. For example, the inherited tendency would be for males to have more than one mate. And it is still true that polygamy (many wives to one husband) is much more common than polyandry (many husbands to one wife). However, polygamous marriages are often difficult, creating much strife among the wives as they compete for their husband's attention and resources. Polygamy also favors social inequity, for the men who acquire more wives are those with greater wealth and power. So the majority of people have instituted enforced monogamy, which offers a more equal relationship and reduces conflicts among women and among men.

Work and Resources

*E*ven given the expendability and fragility of the male (see Notes section), men in virtually every society have held and continue to hold the most powerful and respected positions. Why? Are males "naturally" dominant? Are they actually smarter? Recent studies have not supported either contention.

Perhaps control of a society's most valued resources determines who dominates. For example, human beings need protein to live, and meat is a much more concentrated source of protein than are fruits and vegetables. Men are the ones who hunt for this high-value resource (as is explained shortly). A large gazelle, caught and brought home by a hunting party, can feed several families for several days; thus, many can eat well for a long period of time from the labor of a few.

An alternative theory is that women's reproductive potential is the most valuable resource of all, and males' need to control this potential may actually lead to male domination. For men need to be able to identify their offspring so as to be sure that their investment is worth it, genetically speaking; females always know who their baby is, but males can never be sure unless they dominate sexual access to a particular female. So, in order to be secure about one's children, one must first secure the woman involved. And women would support this in order to find mates who will invest in their children.

Men dominate and claim high status work, too, but in a different way. In all of the eight hundred preindustrial societies that anthropologists have studied, men hunt and women gather, in part because it is difficult to be an effective hunter while pregnant or while nursing or carrying a child. Also, males are physically bigger and stronger than females and are usually faster runners.

Males do the fighting in every society. This is not only because of their greater physical strength but also because it again acts to ensure the survival of the next generation. In a population of a hundred males and a hundred females, if ninety-nine females died in battle, there would probably be only one child born to the group in the next year, and the survival of the population would be in peril. But if ninety-nine men died in battle, the surviving females could each produce a child in the next year with the one remaining man. Thus, males are the more expendable sex in terms of their value for reproduction. Their seed is plentiful and cheap, while women's is limited and dear to the race.[3]

However, people don't view each other exclusively as baby machines. Buss found that in all parts of the world, people value qualities like kindness, understanding, and intelligence more highly in a prospective mate than earning power and attractiveness. There was no male-female difference in this; both sexes wish to share their lives with bright, good-natured people.

_____

3. This analysis assumes, of course, a condition when maximal reproduction would be most advantageous. Today, with large-scale overpopulation, exuberant reproduction is no longer adaptive.

The sex differences in areas beyond sexuality that cannot be accounted for by socialization practices seem to have their roots in hormonal effects on brain development. In lower mammals, the relationship between behavior, ability, and hormones is much more clearly definable than in humans. Male hormones cause rats of both sexes to exhibit increased aggression, faster maze learning, and to assume the male sexual posture during mating. Lack of male hormones causes them to adopt the female sexual posture, learn mazes more slowly, and be less aggressive. Male rats seem to use spatial cues in learning mazes more than the females do, which accounts for their speed advantage. Further, the administration of hormones to rats affects their brain development.

In general, sex hormones play a much more prominent role in the behavior of nonhuman mammals than in humans. Given the tiny differences in cognitive ability between men and women, it seems unlikely that these differences have served any role in the evolutionary success of humans. Their existence may instead be simply a by-product of hormonal effects on brain structure. For instance, some brain structures are modified by fetal exposure to testosterone. The left hemisphere develops more slowly than the right and is therefore more at risk for adverse influences. Testosterone may further slow left-hemisphere development, resulting in relatively greater right-hemisphere dominance. Support for this idea can be seen in the fact that there are more left-handed men than women.

Studies of right- versus left-handed people show that there is a connection between brain organization and spatial ability. Left-handed women seem to be better at spatial skills than right-handed women, and left-handed men seem to be worse at spatial skills than right-handed men. There are no stereotypes that could explain how cultural experiences could create the opposite tendency in spatial ability in right- versus left-handed men and women. So this finding is a good indication that visuospatial ability is biologically affected rather than purely social in origin.

There are recent and interesting results regarding hormonal effects on spatial abilities. In spatial tests, men with low testosterone levels perform better than those with high levels, and the opposite is true for women. Thus, there seems to be an optimum level of testosterone for spatial skills.

There is some evidence that it is not testosterone but the "female" hormone estradiol that controls differences in spatial competence. Testosterone is actually converted to estradiol before it acts in the brain. Females, who naturally produce estradiol in addition to small amounts of testosterone, have much more brain estradiol than men do. The theory here is that both high and low estradiol levels are correlated with relatively poor spatial ability. There seems to be a happy middle level of the hormone that correlates with high spatial ability. The best levels are found in women who produce more testosterone than average and in men who produce less than average. Thus, maleness and femaleness are not the issue at all. The important thing is the level of hormone production, independent of sex.

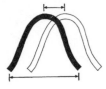

Support for this idea comes out of research showing that women's abilities fluctuate with the hormonal variations of their menstrual cycle. Indeed, when "female" hormones are lowest, at menstruation, women do better on spatial tasks. When estrogen is high at midphase, women are more verbally fluent and articulate. These differences are very small, however. And it is worth mentioning that men show fluctuations, too, although over longer periods of time. For example, Canadian psychologist Doreen Kimura found that male spatial skills are enhanced in the springtime when their testosterone levels are low.

Visuospatial Ability

*V*isuospatial ability refers to skill in representing, transforming, generating, and recalling symbolic, nonlinguistic information. This set of skills is very important in fields such as engineering, architecture, chemistry, and construction. Tests of visuospatial ability are used to predict a student's success in engineering courses. Differences in this ability represent the strongest sex differences except for those involving sexuality itself.

Consider the results of standardized tests, like the SAT, taken by thousands of students over the past twenty-seven years. By 1983, boys had closed the long-time gap on tests of language skill and reduced by 50 percent earlier differences in perceptual speed. Girls had also narrowed the gap considerably in tests of spatial and numerical skills. Only in test scores on the highest levels of mathematics, where visuospatial skills come strongly into play, did differences continue to persist, with males scoring better than females. And we can't overlook the influence of males doing much more math course work on tests of advanced math.[4]

There are differences in the way men and women visualize themselves in space. Men are good at imagining themselves rotating an object or manipulating it. They are good at navigating through a planned route. Women are not inferior in spatial abilities overall, but they are superior only at certain sorts of things; they picture the route more by landmarks, for example, than by abstract directions.

Men and women thus learn routes very differently. Lisa Galea studied undergraduates who were asked to follow a route on a map. Men learned the route much more quickly than women did. But once both men and women had learned it, women remembered the route more by using landmarks than did men. Men seemed to have a superior skill at analyzing the space in terms of abstract ideas, while women seemed to be better at remembering how space is actually organized. Perhaps these differences have to do with the way in which men and women evolved in the days before industry or agriculture.

In hunter-gatherer societies, there was a marked division of labor, and these different spatial abilities may have had some selective advantage. Men were responsible for hunting game, which often required long-distance travel, and for defending the group; both skills involved going into new territory that had not previously been mapped. Men might well, then, have evolved an ability to find long-distance routes—an ability that would allow them to recognize a geographic array from varying orientations, and, some say, to find other women and father the "extra" child.

It may also have been an advantage for women, who would necessarily stay closer to camp, to be better at remembering local signs. Women would have required a short-range navigational ability that used landmarks, and they would have needed fine

---

4. It is possible that we could add to the ranks of brilliant mathematicians by offering training in visuospatial skills as part of formal education. Significant relationships exist between mathematical achievement and visuospatial abilities. In fact, when researchers have examined the relationships of spatial ability to quantitative ability and sex, they have found that spatial skills make all the difference and that sex is irrelevant.

motor capacities for use in the limited space close to home. But maybe not; perhaps the difference is an accidental by-product of the hormones in utero, and societies merely took advantage of it.

Development of Boys and Girls

*B*oys show earlier right-hemisphere development than do girls. (Remember that the right hemisphere connects to the left hand, eye, and ear and that the left hemisphere connects to the right.) Psychologist Sandra Witelson asked boys and girls ages three to thirteen years old to match held objects to viewed shapes. At age five, boys did better with objects held in the left hand than with those held in their right. Girls did not show a similar superiority until age thirteen.

Girls are slightly better than boys at left-hemisphere tasks. Marcia Bryden presented spoken syllables to boys and girls in kindergarten, second, fourth, sixth, and eighth grades. By the fourth grade, the girls showed a right-ear (left-hemisphere) advantage on listening tasks; boys were slower in developing their left-hemisphere abilities.

Like adult men, boys do better at locating the horizontal or vertical in a distracting background, and they're better at "mental rotation," the ability to turn or unfold an image mentally in order to recognize the same shape from a different vantage point. They are also better at "time-of-arrival" tasks, which measure the ability to judge correctly when a moving object will strike a target.

Verbal Skills

*D*ifferences between men and women in verbal skills are much smaller than those related to sexuality and spatial abilities. Females test better than males do on verbal skills, such as grammar, spelling, reading, verbal analogy solving, vocabulary, word generation on demand, and oral comprehension. The difference shows up best in "associational fluency"—the ability to think of synonyms to words. Males do slightly better with verbal analogies (for example, "Sock is to foot as glove is to ——————"), which could explain why boys tend to do a little better on the verbal section of the Scholastic Aptitude Test, despite the general female verbal advantage shown on other tests.

*L*ike most animals, human males are consistently more aggressive than females. Males engage in more rough-and-tumble play; they use more physical aggression. They try to dominate peers and engage in more antisocial behavior than women do. Males prefer television programs with more aggressive content. They also are more active and exploratory than females. They have more accidents requiring emergency medical treatment than females do. And they perceive themselves as more daring and adventurous. Males are more impulsive and more mischievous than females. They are more likely to have temper tantrums, engage in disruptive behaviors, and overreact to frustration.

*S*ocially, females are more likely to be fearful, anxious, and less self-confident than males. They have a less favorable attitude toward their own competence, score higher on measures of social desirability, and are more compliant. In group situations characterized by uncertainty, they are more influenced by peer pressure than males are.

Women are more empathetic than men. Their friendships, in our culture at least, emphasize discussions of feelings, and they are more accurate in reading a person's emotions from facial expressions and tone of voice than males are. They are more involved in prosocial activities, like educating the disadvantaged and feeding the homeless, while men engage more than women in political and social dissent, such as protesting the Vietnam war.

Friendship patterns also differ. Women develop more intensive social relations than men, who have more numerous and less involved relationships. In all cultures, women express more interest in babies and engage in more nurturing activities.

*M*ales (on the average) show an advantage over females in mathematical tasks. If "math ability" is broken down into different types, however, males excel in the areas of math that require visuospatial abilities, such as geometry, while females do better at understanding mathematical sentences, a skill that uses verbal processes.

At least in grade school, girls are better than boys at calculation. However, on the SAT—which is all-important for college admissions and career opportunities—the average boy's score has been consistently about fifty points higher than the average girl's. But most of this average difference occurs at the top of the scale. Of those scoring above 700 (out of 800), there are seventeen boys for every girl. For those achieving average scores in the 400s, there are no such dramatic differences. This means that the average boy is not much likelier to be good at math than the average girl, but a math genius is much more likely to be a male.

Self-Esteem

*P*arents in our culture encourage boys more in math, and boys enroll in more advanced math courses than girls do. During adolescence (seventh to twelfth grade), males gain an average of 1.62 IQ points while females lose an average of 1.33. This is alarming! The researcher who found this result hypothesized that girls apparently "lose intelligence" as the result of efforts to conform to female stereotypes. Supporting this, the girls who declined in their scores behaved more stereotypically female than those who maintained their IQ; however, biological explanations might still hold here.

Consider, also, a study of ratios of male and female "gifted" children. In elementary school, the ratio is fifty-fifty. By junior high, less than 25 percent of the "gifted" group is female. If sex-role stereotypes are responsible for this change, then we are losing a quarter of our highly talented potential contributors to society to the misbegotten notion that it is not "feminine" to be intelligent.

Parents' Influence on Sex Roles

*O*ur first words spoken about a baby are about its sex. "It's a girl!" or "It's a boy!" we exclaim. From the first moments of life, sex has important influences on identity, behavior, and personality. There are a few obvious behavioral differences between boys and girls at birth: newborn boys are more active than girls; they are awake more and grimace more. They are more irritable, as well.

But cultural influence begins at the moment of birth and, nowadays, even before birth, with the first ultrasound. Whether boys or girls wear pink clothes and lace or play with toy trucks and guns is not determined by genetics or hormones. These are cultural choices. By age five, a child is aware of sex differences and strives to emulate same-sex models: parents, other children, and people on television.

As early as one day after a baby's birth, parents are likely to judge their sons as being strong, firm, and hardy and their daughters as soft, small, and delicate, although such differences do not yet exist. Parents interpret a baby boy's cry more often as anger and a girl's as fear, since they interpret a male as aggressive and a girl as timid.

The parents, surprisingly, are often unaware of the bias: a study found that mothers handled a six-month-old baby differently if they had heard that it was a boy than if they thought it was a girl (it was a boy). After the experiment, they denied that their actions were different in the two situations.

But the different treatment makes a difference: at one year of age, boys and girls are equally happy with a doll or a truck. But parents typically give girls dolls, dollhouses, and stuffed animals, while boys get blocks, trucks, and sports equipment. By age three, children begin to show a clear preference for toys "appropriate" to their gender.

Parents also play with their infant sons and daughters differently. Mothers touch their little girls more and prefer to keep them close by; they speak to their infant daughters more frequently and longer than they do to their sons. By age two, girls generally prefer to play closer to their mothers than do boys. Little boys are more likely to be tossed, swung, and chased. In most cultures, they are also more likely than girls to be aggressive and to get into confrontations. The parents of boys are also more concerned with discipline and with pushing their child toward achievement than are the parents of girls.

Fathers influence sex roles in their children more than do mothers. Fathers are more likely to reward their daughters for playing with other girls but punish their sons for playing with girls.

It's not only parents who convey social influence; the children do so themselves. Shortly after children can identify their own sex, they prefer same-sex social partners, even if adults encourage mixed-sex play. By the age of four, little girls prefer to play with other girls and little boys with other boys. In fact, children who do have opposite-sex play partners often choose to keep the friendship a secret. Strong sex segregation persists until adolescence when heterosexual action starts.

Children learn from the people they observe which behaviors are good and bad. They identify with same-sex models and adopt "female" or "male" behavior according to what they see. For instance, one study found that girls who had mothers who worked outside the home displayed more flexibility in their personal sex roles, presumably because they had seen their mothers acting in different roles.

Role Models

Nowadays, the major source of role models is television. By age four, the average child has watched more than two thousand hours of TV! Gender stereotypes are very strongly portrayed in television dramas and commercials. According to psychologist Diane Halpern, on television, "men and boys are shown as active, hardworking, goal-oriented individuals, whereas women and girls are depicted as housewives and future housewives." The men are "dominant, aggressive, autonomous, and active," while the women are "passive and defiant."

Social influences on the development of sex roles begin at birth and perhaps before it. Thus, in reflecting on the meaning of biologically driven differences between men and women, we should keep in mind that experiences themselves can alter the workings of the human brain. This will be discussed in Chapter Sixteen.

Schooling

The few consistent differences in mental abilities could easily result from differences in experience. Once children enter school, you might think that instructors would teach all of them without concern for their sex. However, teachers do not treat boys and girls equally in the classroom, and like parents, they are unaware of this bias.

A three-year study of fourth, sixth, and eighth graders in several states showed that teachers praised boys more than girls, and they paid more attention to boys. Teachers also gave boys better answers to their questions. Part of this dominance of boys in the classroom may result from boys' greater tendency to grab attention and call out unsolicited answers, greater innate male aggressiveness.

In both males and females, exposure to male hormones before birth leads to more aggressive play styles. While scientists cannot give hormones to human beings to find out if the administration of these hormones would affect development, accidental events can sometimes illuminate these relationships. For instance, a recessive genetic disorder called congenital adrenal hyperplasia (CAH) results in the adrenal glands releasing abnormally large quantities of androgens (hormones) in the third week of fetal development.

Although called "male" hormones, androgens are present at lower levels in females, too. CAH girls engage in more "aggressive play." In the 1950s, it was not uncommon to give pregnant women synthetic sex hormones to prevent miscarriage. This produced a set of females and males exposed to extremely high prenatal androgen levels. The children, both female and male, who had been exposed to the excess sex hormones in the womb were more aggressive than those who had not. Fifty-seven percent of CAH males show above-average aggression, while 43 percent of the females do.

There are, then, some consistent, though minor, sex-related differences. But whenever this topic of biologically determined differences between male and female aptitudes comes up, there is an outcry of protest from many socially concerned individuals. They have a well-grounded fear that noting or focusing on any of these differences will thwart ongoing attempts to end discrimination against women. And, indeed, there are always people who will distort research findings to serve bigoted ends. Diane Halpern expressed the concern well in *Sex Differences in Cognitive Abilities:*

> It is frightening . . . to consider the possibility that even a small portion of the sex differences in cognitive abilities may be attributable to biological factors. This is probably because many people confuse biological

The Importance of Sex Difference Findings

contributions with the idea of an immutable or unavoidable destiny. Suppose . . . I conclude that males really are superior in mathematics and that sex-differentiated hormones or brain organization are implicated in these differences. This does not necessarily reduce the importance of psychosocial variables, nor does it imply that the differences are large or that the differences could not be reduced or eliminated with appropriate instruction. What such a conclusion does do, however, is create the potential for misquotation, misuse, and misinterpretation. Perhaps the very publication of such research results creates a considerable risk.

The real importance in sex-difference findings is hinted at in Halpern's statement. If it were known that men or women have, at birth, a disparity in certain skills, then we could develop training programs to enhance these skills. Keep in mind that the revelation of sex-related differences does not necessarily mean female deficiency. When millions of scores are averaged, we find that females do slightly better at some tasks, and males do slightly better at others.

Almost all mental differences between men and women are products of social processes that we can alter, if we choose, to ensure that each individual is encouraged to develop her or his abilities to the full. In the modern world, biological differences matter little.

After all, what is important and what lies behind these gender differences? First I want to reassert that the differences are extremely small and far outweighed by our great similarity. Individual mental ability varies greatly; there is a much larger difference between a man of poor ability and one of high ability or between a woman of poor ability and one of high ability than there is between an average man and an average woman. When assessing individuals for aptitudes and the need for special instructional attention, we should only consider their actual demonstrated capacity.

Sexual identity tells us nothing about individual mental ability. Perhaps some differences exist as of the moment, but they will continue to decrease as opportunities for education and advancement even out. As society offers women more and more control over their resources, the historical role of the male in "providing" will become less and less necessary, and the male dominance in many parts of life will decrease and disappear eventually.

However, I believe that the differences in mating strategy and sexual style that are closely allied to pregnancy or sperm production will never completely disappear. These differences, unlike racial ones, are deep roots of the human self. Still, even in this arena, biology no longer creates our destiny. And as we consider other components of the self, moving further away from sexuality, our biological nature matters less and less.

Part Four

Differences in Mind

Chapter 13

The Hand, the Brain, and the Individual Mind

*L*eft-handers are a minority, but they are everywhere. They comprise about a tenth of the population worldwide. They face difficulty living in a right-handed world; it is sometimes difficult for left-handers to write alphabet languages because these were designed by and for right-handers—even most school desks present an awkward problem for left-handers.

Handedness is significant to our individuality because of the way the two halves of the brain are specialized. Thus, in the "normal pattern"—that is, in most right-handed people—language and other sequential abilities mostly involve the left hemisphere. Spatial abilities and simultaneous thinking reside primarily in the right hemisphere. In left-handed people, however, brain organization can be different.

In 1982, my colleagues (Dr. David Galin and Jeannine Herron) and I at the Langley-Porter Neuropsychiatric Institute in San Francisco carried out a large electroencephalographic (EEG) study of left-handers. As mentioned in Chapter Eight, Galin and I had, a decade earlier, developed a method of recording the activation and idling of the hemispheres through scalp recordings.

In recording left-handers doing pretty ordinary things like writing, singing, or calculating, we found three types of hemispheric organization: (1) those whose cortical organization is similar to right-handers, (2) those whose organization is reversed, and (3) those who have language and spatial abilities in both hemispheres.

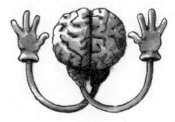

There is controversy regarding whether being left-handed affects intellectual abilities and what the differences in brain organization might mean. Further, some important claims have been made in regard to lefties' longevity, intelligence, and thought processes.

Some left-handers have both sides of their brain controlling language, as we found with our EEG study and as others have found using sodium amytal injected into one hemisphere or the other. Some researchers find that left-handers have less spatial ability than right-handers, but while this may be true on average, how could we, then, account for Leonardo da Vinci? Or the fact that more architects are left-handed than is their percentage in the general population?

There is a cultural bias against things of the left. The English word *gauche* (meaning "awkward" or "in poor taste") is nothing but the French word for left, while the Latin word for left *(sinistra)* has become our word *sinister*. The Maoris of New Zealand are even more specific: the right is the "side of life" (and of strength), according to them, while the left is "the side of death" (and of weakness).

And left-handers have never gotten good press. The very word *left* comes from the Anglo-Saxon *lyft,* which means "weak" or "broken"; dictionary definitions of left-handed include "awkward," "clumsy," "ill-omened," and "inauspicious." Left-handers are pressured at school to write with their right hands, and they inhabit a world where everything—scissors, jugs, corkscrews, most gadgets and machinery—is designed for right-handers. Some even advocate a Left-hander Liberation Front to put their cause on the social-consciousness map. While there is little sign of this happening at the moment, it is true that left-handers are still viewed as negatively as in Anglo-Saxon times.

Being Left-Handed

To understand what being left-handed means, we need to ask why there are left-handers, anyway. In all other species, including the chimpanzees, individual animals favor their left or right side on a fifty-fifty basis. One study observed thirty-one captive lowland gorillas to determine which paw they used to reach for food, and found a full range of "hand preferences" between strong left and strong right, with most animals showing intermediate levels of preference. Most animals were very consistent, too.

However, human beings strongly favor not only the right hand (nine out of ten) but also the right foot (eight out of ten), the right eye (seven out of ten), and the right ear (six out of ten). Females are more strongly "right-eous": 90–91 percent of women are right-handers while only 86–87 percent of men are. However, handedness isn't absolute: some right-handers (13 percent) have a stronger grip with the left hand, while over half of left-handers grip better with their right.

When did the tendency toward right-handedness first emerge? It is impossible to say exactly at what moment early human beings became left-brain, right-hand dominant, but some research suggests that we have favored that side for hundreds of thousands of years. One study of over a thousand pictures that were drawn between 15,000 B.C. and 1950 and that showed people doing something with their hands found that 93 percent portrayed the use of the right. A microscopic analysis of prehistoric tools dating back two hundred thousand years showed that about 80 percent of them were worn more heavily on the right, indicating right-hand use. Further back, we have evidence of two-million-year-old skulls of baboons believed to have been clubbed to death by a person or persons unknown, but probably early humans, using the right hand.

The long history of left-handedness indicates that something important is in operation to dispose 10 percent of the population throughout the world to prefer the left. Left-handedness could be genetic like blond hair, a trait that is less common because both parents have to have the gene for it to be passed on. A look at the Kerr family from Scotland, a clan famous for breeding left-handers, supports this view.

The proportion of left-handers among Kerr family members is indeed remarkable: 29.5 percent are left-handed compared to 10 percent in the general population. The family owns a large group of castles and manor houses, all of which have staircases that spiral round to the left. They were designed in this way so that a left-handed swordsman would have the advantage when retreating up the stairs before a right-handed attacker. The family's fighting skill and left-handedness were even celebrated in a ballad:

"But the Kerrs were aye the deadliest foes/That e'er to English-men were known/For they were all bred left-handed men/And fence against them there was none." (Left-handed swordsmen still have the advantage even without a special spiral staircase: at the Moscow Olympics, the top fencers were all left-handers.)

Both parents influence left-handedness, but not equally. Many studies, such as a big one of two thousand families in Canada, have revealed that having a left-handed mother doubles your chances of being left-handed, while the handedness of the father seems to have no effect. Even if both parents are lefties—the optimum condition for passing on a genetic trait—the child's chances of being a left-hander are only three or four times greater than normal.

Even identical twins have only about an 85 percent chance of having the same handedness, just slightly more than the chance (78 percent) that any two unrelated individuals will have the same handedness. But genetics do matter in the strength of handedness (measured by how many of about a dozen different tasks, like writing or throwing a ball, are done with one hand). Strong left-handers will have strongly handed children, although they could be left-handed or right-handed.

As long ago as 1686, a philosopher observed that left-handedness was a "digression or aberration from the way which nature generally intendeth." In 1913 an American popular science magazine observed: "A sound and capable stock, like a right-handed one, breeds true generation after generation. Then something slips a cog, and there appears a left-handed child, a black sheep, or an imbecile."

Left-handedness, however, comes not from a slipped cog but from the brain. The suggestion is often made that in left-handers something has gone "wrong" with the way brain connections are made. And, for some, this is the case. In almost any group of people with psychological problems, there *are* more left-handers than normal. A study in Great Britain in 1921 found that while 7 percent of the children in regular schools were left-handed, 18 percent were in schools for mentally retarded children. More schizophrenics are left-handed, and their mental impairment is worse than that of the right-handed ones. The strongest connection, however, is with dyslexia. Left-handers are twelve times more likely to be dyslexic than right-handers. Epileptics, alcoholics, depressives, drug addicts, and insomniacs all have more than their fair share of left-handers.

Fortunately, the pathological left-hander isn't the only one. What about the many left-handers who are pretty good or even excellent at what they do? They have been the life's work of Dr. Marian Annett at the University of Leicester in England, who began studying left-handers over twenty years ago because she was struck by the greater-than-average number of them who were highly intelligent.

The Handedness Continuum

*W*hile we tend to think of people as either righties or lefties, hand preferences are actually on a continuum from strong left to strong right. Annett proposes a theory about the origin of hand preferences in which three factors are involved. The first is accidental variation in the development of the two sides of the body. The second is a systematic bias to the right hand in human beings, probably linked with the tendency of the left hemisphere to serve speech. The third consists of social and cultural influences that affect the expression of leftwardness, as when a child is trained to conform to the majority by switching hands.

Here's how Annett's "right-shift" theory works. For our close relatives, the chimpanzees, handedness is a matter of chance; for human beings, that chance element is still there, but there's a unique factor—there is one human gene that gives a bias to the left brain (controlling the right side), making it more likely that speech and language will develop there. So while there is a genetic element in handedness, it isn't a gene for right-handedness per se. Being right-handed is just a by-product of the evolution of the left brain for controlling language.

What happens, Annett supposes, is this: about 50 percent of the population receive this left-brain-bias gene (LBBG) from one parent and become mildly right-handed. About 30 percent get the gene from both parents (LBBG2) and go on to be strong right-handers. Finally, about 20 percent don't have the LBBG, and their handedness is decided just as it is for chimps—entirely at random. This means that half of that 20 percent (that is, 10 percent) would be left-handed, which is indeed the percentage of left-handers in the overall population that most studies find. Left-handedness, then, develops naturally and at random when the genetic bias to the left brain is missing.

The **LBBG** must give people an advantage or it wouldn't be so common, so it's not surprising that mild right-handers are better at developing speech and language than *either left-handers or strong right-handers*. The problems for the **LBBG2** types (who receive the gene from both parents) result from the way **LBBG** works, which is not by beefing up the left brain but by downgrading the right brain.

Not only do right-handers have fewer brain cells in the corpus callosum (the bridge between the left and right sides) but parts of the right brain are smaller, too. Annett's studies in schools find that the more strongly right-handed someone is, the weaker and less skillful their left hand. The same isn't true for left-handers; strong left-handers don't have much weaker right hands.

This suggests that being strongly right-handed indicates a reduction in the ability of the right brain, with no compensating improvement of the left brain. Annett looked at the relationships among arithmetic ability, hand preference, and hand skill in schoolchildren aged nine to eleven years. The weaker the right-handedness, the better the children were at arithmetic.

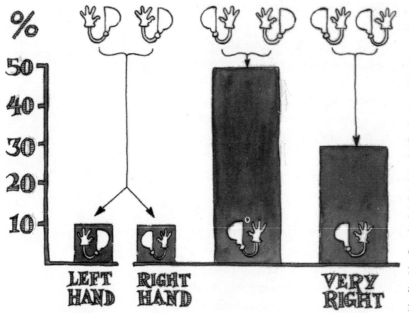

While shifting to the right hand and left hemisphere has had great advantages, like the emergence of language, the human right-handed bias has been achieved at a cost—a reduction in the efficiency of left-sided actions. Thus, many scientists have assumed that *all* left-handers have problems. However, this simply isn't true. While there is a group of left-handers who have more troubles in learning and coordination, Annett finds, surprisingly, that "normal" left-handers have fewer deficiencies in learning and intelligence than the strongly right-handed. Not all left-handers have a weakened right brain, as do the right-handers, and these normal lefties do better at a wide range of tasks, with the exception of the early development of language.

The right-shift (RS) theory suggests that the human bias to the right is a trade-off: give a system a language boost, and you may lose spatial skills. It also explains why right dominance hasn't taken over completely, which is what you would expect if it were an unmixed blessing, and it explains all those left-handers who excel.

Annett sampled children from six primary schools, individually testing them for hand preference, hand skill, and Raven's Matrices, a nonverbal intelligence test. The rightmost children were poorer than all others on the matrices, verbal skills, and several other tests. Strong dexterity was associated with weak left hand skill, not good right hand skill, in accord with the hypothesis that the costs of RS are to the right hemisphere, which interferes less with the left.

Left-handers were superior at mathematics. This fits in with a weakening of the right brain by LBBG2, since mathematical ability has been described as "a language to describe those aspects of human experience that are otherwise understood only in visuospatial images"—in other words, math skills make strong use of the right side of the brain. The effect Annett found was small but consistent: for both boys and girls, the more strongly right-handed pupils were, the worse they did on intelligence and other test scores.

Studies of twins confirm the right-shift theory. Even when twins have the LBBG, it only means there is a *bias* to the left brain; the choice still has a random element. Without the gene (non-LBBG), the choice is totally random—remember that the probability of twins sharing handedness is only a bit higher than that of two unrelated people.

In the analysis of schizophrenia, I proposed that a little "liberation" may lead to creative gains while too much may lead to disorders. Similarly, the existence of left-handers is vital for the gene pool, since it would be disastrous if everyone had only the LBBG. Without left-handers, there would be many more LBBG2 types around, and as Annett found, they perform rather badly at intellectual and learning tasks. Annett suggests that the reason left-handers are more likely to be good at chess and math and are bright generally is not because they have something that improves them but because the LBBG2 makes people worse.

This is still only a theory, but it explains well some of the puzzling features of left-handers, and it links our brain development with our primate ancestors. They get left- or right-handedness in a genetic lottery, and the idea that the lottery is still working in us, only with a bias to one side, seems much more likely than the suggestion that we, of all the mammals, have been reprogrammed to be right-sided. Evolution is cost-conscious, and new pieces, like a gene that gives a push to the left brain, tend to be tacked onto what's already there, rather than installing a whole new system.

What is most notable, after all of Annett's extensive testing of schoolchildren, is just how little difference there is between normal left- and right-handers. All of the tendencies—being better or worse at math and languages—exist when you look at a large number of pupils, but individual left- or right-handers may be very similar in all sorts of ways. It is the extremes that make the groupings appear different. Thus, if you are a lefty and pretty normal in most things, there is little reason to think that your temperament or personality will be especially different from that of a right-hander. In terms of a career, architecture or fencing might be a slightly better bet than linguistic philosophy, but such advice could just as well fit a strong right-hander.

Pathology and Left-handedness

There are difficulties presented by being left-handed in a right-handed world. Signs and controls on machinery are designed for righties. The shift lever on the car falls naturally to the right hand, not the left, which may contribute to the extra car accidents that lefties experience. Industrial tools, too, are designed for righties.

Left-handers make more use of the greater ability of the right side of their brain to deal with spatial perception; art students, for instance, are more likely to be left-handers and ambidextrous—47 percent lefty or ambi as opposed to 22 percent for students in general. In one architecture school, 29 percent of the students were left-handed, and 73 percent of them finished the course as opposed to 62 percent of the right-handers.

So does being left-handed signify no more than that one will be mildly inconvenienced by scissors and corkscrews? Are left-handers falsely derided as weak and incompetent? Well, yes and no.

Pathology and Left-handedness

What has given lefties a bad name is that some of them have sustained different kinds of brain damage. Some become left-handed as a result of birth trauma, which affects other systems and interferes with longevity. If the hemispheres are bruised during the trip through the narrow birth canal, a natural right-hander is more likely to become a lefty than the reverse. Some lefties have become so because of damage to the left hemisphere. All left-handers have a different brain organization from righties, which affects control of language and movement, and may disorganize many immune and cardiac functions, perhaps leading to their greater susceptibility to disease.

Thus, there are different sources of left-handedness—some harmless, some pathological. This explains how there can be both so many potential problems associated with being left-handed and how there can be a large proportion of left-handers who have no problems at all. Grouped together, however, lefties show an *average* disadvantage in comparison to righties. For natural, mild left-handers it is no more significant than having a birth mark or slender fingers.

Part of the explanation for this is that because left-handers are rare anyway, it only takes a fairly small percentage of right-handers being switched over by birth difficulties to double their number. The other part has to do with the way handedness is controlled in the brain.

There are as many as twenty-three brain centers involved in controlling our hands, and they are spread all over the brain, from the cerebral cortex (which is involved in the higher sorts of thinking) to the spinal cord (which is concerned with reflex actions), and it seems that damage to any one of those centers can produce a switch from right- to left-handedness.

This is why left-handedness seems to be associated with such a wide range of problems: the damage that produces the left-to-right brain switch can occur in an awful lot of places, and wherever it occurs, it may affect other abilities that are controlled by the same area. Consequently, being a left-hander isn't a problem in itself, but for one subset of these individuals, it is a sign that something, somewhere, may have gone wrong in the brain.

In other words, it is likely that there are two sorts of left-handers—natural and pathological. The natural ones, who are in the majority (although no one is sure of their exact percentage of the total), are organized to be left-handed, but the pathological ones are right-handers in whom some damage occurred to the left brain during birth or during development. Thus, the right brain has become dominant in these individuals, with left-handedness as the result.

The left brain is more at risk even in the womb. The right hemisphere develops first, while the left develops later and more slowly so that it's more vulnerable to damage. If too much testosterone is produced, it can slow down development. Then, during birth, because of the normal position of the baby's head, the blood supply to the left brain is more likely to be temporarily cut off. Any damage of this sort to the left brain can cause a switch to the right brain and so produce a left-hander.

And this is where the effect of pregnancy and birth on creating left-handers comes in. It is fairly well established that many of the problems of left-handers—being retarded, schizophrenic, or alcoholic —are connected with difficulties at the time of birth—caesareans, breech births, forceps deliveries, being premature, and so on. The first person to research the connection was Paul Bakan in 1973; his claim that *all* left-handedness might be the result of birth difficulties caused an outrage, since it implied that all left-handers were brain damaged. As we have seen, this is not true.

There's a strong sex difference, too: males are much more likely to be affected by complications at birth and are more likely to be left-handed as a result of prolonged labor, breech birth, low birth weight, caesarean delivery, multiple births, or Rh incompatibility (mother and baby being of a different Rh blood group). Females are likely to switch handedness if they experience the following difficulties: premature birth, prolonged labor, breathing difficulty, or multiple births. Overall, premature babies are five times more likely to be left-handed, and older mothers, who are more likely to have complications anyway, give birth to more left-handers: for pregnant women between the ages of thirty and thirty-four, lefty babies are nearly 20 percent more likely than earlier births; between thirty-five and thirty-nine, that proportion jumps to 69 percent, and over forty, it reaches 128 percent.

These birth traumas leave the left-hander much more vulnerable: they are twice as likely to have sleep problems, twice as likely to be cross-eyed, two and a half times more likely to be deaf. Most at risk seems to be their immune system, which may be damaged by too much testosterone while in the womb; testosterone, as well as harming the left brain, can also attack the thymus gland—a crucial part of the body's defenses.

People with a damaged thymus are far more likely to suffer from allergies like hay fever and asthma. A study in Glasgow in 1982 found that left-handers were eleven and a half times more likely to have hay fever, asthma, and eczema, and an allergy clinic in London found that their patients were 70 percent more likely to be left-handed. American research has found that twice as many migraine sufferers are lefties.

Similar but even more dangerous than allergies are the autoimmune diseases in which the body starts to treat its own proteins as hostile. Left-handed males are particularly prone to diabetes, while the connection with left-handed females is not so clear. On the other hand, Crohn's disease (which affects the small intestine) is three times more likely in left-handed females than in right-handed ones.

Brain damage may also slow normal growth. A sign of how fast someone is developing is the age at which they reach puberty; 75 percent of North American women have had a period by the age of fourteen, and 75 percent of the males have begun to grow a beard and have pubic hair by the age of sixteen. But left-handers tend to get there later—at fourteen, only 40 percent of left-handed females have had a period, and at sixteen, only 43 percent of the males have an adult body hair pattern.

Thus, the ripples from early brain damage spread out: left-handed males are four times more susceptible to brain damage than their right-handed counterparts and less likely to respond to treatment; left-handers are more likely to be smokers and take other drugs. According to recordings of brain wave patterns, left-handers seem to be more affected by drugs than right-handers.

It is not surprising that left-handers are three times more prone to depression and suicide, but it is puzzling that the children of depressives are six times more likely to be left-handed. There is a fascinating case from the end of the last century involving a Welsh sailor who was a manic-depressive; when he was excitable and talkative in his manic phase, he was right-handed, but when he became depressed and withdrawn, he switched to being left-handed. This fits in with the finding that left-handers seem to be more cautious, more affected by stress, and more likely to describe themselves as introverted and aloof than right-handers. And it goes well with the division of emotional expression in the two hemispheres that I presented in Chapter Eight.

All of this evidence that some left-handers are, to a certain degree, brain damaged and therefore likely to be less healthy leads to one claim that has infuriated lefties—on average, they die ten years sooner in the case of men and four years earlier for women. This claim derives in part from an observation made by Stanley Coren; in his twenty years of studying left-handedness, he noticed that while about 13 percent of a group of twenty-year-olds would be left-handed, the proportion had dropped to 5 percent by age fifty and 1 percent by age eighty.

Coren tested the obvious explanation for the "disappearing southpaw"—that pressure to learn to write with the right hand at school or simply the grind of living in a right-handed world gradually caused most left-handers to switch at some point in their lives. Although he found that there was certainly a lot of school pressure—one Catholic-educated man reported a nun declaring, "Every time X uses his left hand, he is doing the devil's work"—Coren also found that the number of left-handers has remained pretty constant throughout this century. He also found that while up to four out of five left-handers can be taught to write right-handed if a determined teacher starts them young enough, these newly right-handed writers still brush their teeth and use scissors with their left hand.

Coren next checked the statistics available on baseball players and found that left-handers at any age had a 2 percent greater chance of dying than righties. He then conducted a study in California that showed that handedness had a greater effect on someone's life expectancy than did their sex.

A contributing factor to lefties' higher mortality rate is undoubtedly their higher accident rate; left-handed students were 89 percent more likely to have accidents that required medical treatment, six times more likely to die from accident-related injuries, and four times more likely to die in a road accident. Yet while this evidence is strong, other studies have not found this striking difference. So although it is unlikely that Coren's findings about left-handers' mortality will prove completely wrong, the size of the difference between lefties and righties may well be less.

*A*ll these gloomy findings might lead us to ask how it happens that there are *any* left-handers who aren't confined to long-stay hospital wards or some other sort of institution. In looking at all these greater risks and threatening percentages, we haven't accounted for the successful left-handers—all three presidential candidates in the 1992 election, for example, were lefties.

There is the connection with architects and art schools, as already mentioned, as well as the link with champion fencers. A few other sports also give left-handers the edge. There is a myth that left-handers dominate baseball, but studies haven't supported this. On the other hand, southpaws in boxing do seem to do better, probably for the same reason that the Kerrs did well at swordplay. People who are ambidextrous have an advantage in basketball and hockey.

One of the most specific left-hander abilities is the set of visuospatial skills. There is a test in psychology in which people are asked to look at an irregular figure—say an "L" shape with an extra projection coming up at right angles from one end—and then to imagine what it would look like in another position. Left-handers do this task better than right-handers, which suggests that they have a better visual imagination—a talent that is useful in physics, chemistry, and engineering, and these are all subjects that, according to one study, have lots of left-handed practitioners. This ability is also useful in chess, and left-handers abound there, too.

The Benefits of Being Left-handed

One more left-hander quality that has already been mentioned in passing—being more extreme in their reaction to drugs—seems to be an example of the tendency in left-handers to be more extreme generally. One study of very bright children in the United States, for example, found that this group contains twice as many left-handers as the general population.

Left-handedness stems from the divided nature of the brain, but it is not the only brain difference that manifests in different abilities. When we look more closely, we can see that the brain is comprised of many different "talents," each one independent of the other, each one contributing to the uniqueness of the self.

Chapter 14

Small Pieces of the Puzzle

Differences in Memory and Thinking

Human beings spend lots of time trying to figure themselves and others out, but our complexity makes self-understanding a difficult venture. We're an unconnected, if not incoherent, mixture of different reactions and tendencies. There are overarching factors in our individuality, such as where we sit on the gain, deliberation-liberation, and approach-withdrawal continua, but they don't seem to correlate well with one another. And none of these factors is associated, either, with family or with whether we're right- or left-handed, male or female.

Moreover, we all have individual "talents"—special-purpose systems that are superior in some, less so in others, just as is the ability to sing beautifully or to play basketball well. The problem lies in determining which of these abilities are central to the self, like, perhaps, the ability to calculate, and which are peripheral, like the ability to curl one's tongue. In this chapter, we will consider many of these smaller pieces of the self.

Consider that the brain is made up of different areas, some of which light up for different functions. While there are group differences—variations between left- and right-handers, between women and men—most of the differences among people do not come from handedness or sex but from a diversity of different "talents."

Much testing has gone on to try to determine a single measure of intelligence. In the last century, some thought that one yardstick was the power of one's handgrip. Nowadays, researchers test memory, language ability, and analytic skills. It is estimated that between three and four million **IQ** tests are administered in this country's schools on a yearly basis. But this test doesn't actually measure "intelligence" (although it does predict school success), and it doesn't teach us much about our nature. Two innovative psychologists, Robert Sternberg and Howard Gardner, are now trying to change the way we measure minds.

Yale psychologist Robert J. Sternberg was given an **IQ** test in the sixth grade. He scored so poorly that he was given the test a second time in the company of fifth-graders. Feeling much more confident now that he was surrounded by his juniors, he triumphed in this second round with an outstanding score. Ever since then (starting in the seventh grade when he created his own version of an **IQ** test for a school science project), he's been designing tests and questioning the validity of standard testing in general.

Even those who don't disapprove of current **IQ** testing believe it is not always an accurate predictor of success. UC Berkeley professor of education Arthur Jensen, who has written several books about the feasibility of **IQ** tests, says of Mensa, an organization for those whose **IQ** scores rank them in the top 2 percent: "They're a strange group. You run into people who have IQs of 160 or so who are college drop-outs and work as elevator operators or parking lot attendants. Their high **IQ** is their only claim to distinction, and they make a lot of it."

Americans have a biased view of intelligence, assuming that it relates to doing well in school and on schoolwork, since most of the tests code for success in schools. But Sternberg, in *The Triarchic Mind*, says, "My claim is not that intelligence is unrelated to schoolwork but rather that it is related to a great deal more." In his

Talents come in different formats

model of intelligence, "mental self-management" is the kind of intelligence that helps people in their day-to-day lives. This kind of intelligence is strategy-based rather than analytically based.

Sternberg divides intelligence into three distinct aspects, and he tests and scores each individually. These aspects are (1) analytical intelligence, which is useful in academic learning; (2) creative intelligence, which is useful for trouble-shooting and for using old ideas or knowledge in new ways; and (3) practical intelligence, which is useful in managing, getting things done, and surviving on the streets of New York.

Most of us are a combination of all three, but each of us is also particularly strong in one of the three. People who are especially successful in the "real world" (who realize their potential and skirt obstacles and interference) take full advantage of their strength in one of these areas, and this ends up compensating for any weaknesses they may have in the other areas.

Howard Gardner has a more expanded view than Sternberg's of the divisions of intelligence; he postulates six major "frames of mind." He believes that the many mental abilities of human beings are separate and potentially independent. These abilities include linguistic intelligence, musical intelligence, logical-mathematical intelligence, and spatial intelligence, the ability that allows you to design and build a table, to assemble a model airplane, to design an office floor plan, or to find your way around town.

Another ability emphasized by Gardner is bodily or kinesthetic intelligence. This ability to use one's body in skilled ways for expressive purposes, as a dancer does, includes the capacity to work skillfully with objects, like an artist does, using the fine motor movements of the fingers and hands. People with a high degree of "body intelligence" may also excel in sports. Again, having this ability does not preclude intelligence in other areas.

Last on Gardner's list is personal intelligence, the ability to read another's feelings and intentions. Human beings are bonded to one another from birth; thus, this ability is very important. Is he angry? we ask ourselves. Will I hurt her if I say that? Is this a good time to ask for a raise? Our survival in the modern world depends on an understanding of other people's intentions and feelings.

Sternberg's and Gardner's ideas have caused much interest in academia and the education world in general, and they may well lead to a better set of tests and education procedures. But I believe that even though they are slightly liberated from the IQ and standard white-rat psychology,[1] they are still focused too closely on an "intellectual" view of our nature.

If we look instead at the different small talents for which there is biological, psychometric, and environmental evidence, then we get a different view of the components of our nature. These components seem to be doled out differently to different individuals and thus can shed light on our sense of self. We've discussed some of the major components in the chapters on temperament. But other minor aspects also mark our individuality.

Thus, instead of thinking of the mind as a single, intellectual entity that can judge many different kinds of events equitably, we should rethink it: the mind is diverse and complex. It contains a changeable selection of different kinds of temperaments and talents—fixed reactions, or general tendencies to react in a certain way—and these different entities are temporarily employed (or as I said in my *Multimind,* "wheeled into consciousness") and then usually discarded after use.

Focus of Mind

Central to the modern analysis of mind is that it is divided into "modules"—separated specialized mechanisms that do specific jobs, such as analyzing visual information, controlling movements, decoding auditory information into language, analyzing smells, and the like. There are distinct modules for different kinds of memory, for example. We all know people who seem to have a good memory for faces but not for numbers. Other people can remember stories well but not directions. "Absentminded professors" may remember specific details of the Peloponnesian War but cannot remember to pick up their laundry. In 1874 Francis Galton, in one of his more rational approaches to individuality, surveyed eminent British men of science as to their means of

---

1. Historically, most psychologists have been middle-class white males. So have the participants in psychological studies. (One text on the history of psychology was aptly titled *Even the Rat Was White.*) Consequently, most of the existing theories of behavior were developed by men, based on studies of men. There is nothing inherently wrong with white men, but there is something wrong with assuming that findings about white men can be generalized to all humans.

working. He found that some relied primarily on vision to remember things, while others relied more on words.

A more recent study under the direction of Ulric Neisser reveals eight separate kinds of memory. The first is rote memory. Some people seem very computerlike in their ability to remember addresses and phone numbers; once they have been given an address, they can recall it forever. Others not only have to write it down but then they have to remember where they wrote it.

Absentmindedness is probably a frontal-lobe function, as are many of the other "keeping-track" activities of the mind. Other frontal-lobe functions involve the ability or inability to recall names; to recognize individuals by their appearance; to remember jokes, stories, and conversations; to know places and where things are. Although these findings are tentative, they suggest that an individual's memory may be assembled out of these components. One person may have a great memory for jokes and names but forget things he or she needs to do. Another may easily remember where things are but have difficulty in remembering why someone's face is familiar. Further research may reveal which of these components of memory are associated with one another.

Talents

I call certain well-defined, anatomically related abilities "talents" because they are to some degree inherited; because some people probably have more of one than another; and because, as in the ability to move gracefully or to speak fluently, they seem to form coherent mental and behavioral units as well as existing as specific anatomical units.

The most biologically similar talents are the *motivators,* located in the centers of the brain that regulate hunger, thirst, and various appetites, from food to sex. These were called "drives" in earlier psychologies. Some people, then, are highly "driven" to succeed at any cost, to become rich, to drink and eat often or well, to have sex. The different kinds of appetites seem to vary among people; we can easily imagine a person strongly dominated by hunger, sex, or thirst.

Fundamental, too, are the *informers;* these abilities are centered in the information-gathering systems of the nervous system. Each of us needs to know what is happening inside and outside.

We need to be able to interpret sounds in the environment, the movement of objects, the position of our own limbs, and especially pain. All of this information must be assembled before we take action, and we need to know what to do with this sensory information. Clearly people differ in how well they perceive what is going on inside and outside themselves: one woman was recently rushed to the hospital in spasms of stomach pain, only to discover that she was about to give birth. She didn't even know that she was pregnant. For others, internal pains and upsets have strong access to consciousness and cannot be ignored. Some people can discriminate between two tones, each of which may be inaudible to a person of average hearing. And sharpshooters often have extraordinary sensory acuity.

Closely associated with the informing talents but most likely the product of separate development is the talent of *smelling*. The physiology of the smell system is certainly anatomically separate from other systems; the nerves from the nose are unique in that they connect directly to the brain without any intermediary synapses. Some people are smell maestros; others are completely indifferent to smell.

The immense job of *moving* involves the coordination of many sights, sounds, colors, tastes, and internal sensations while keeping track of where we are. This ability resides clearly and completely in the central cortex. It consists of a narrow band of specialized neurons that receive the information from the senses and transform the information into movements; this narrow band is often called the "sensory-motor strip." When we watch a baby who is learning to walk, we are reminded of what a huge task such body movement is; the brain must coordinate the movement of one arm, then a leg, then the other one, and all the while we are alternately looking into the distance and down at our feet. Some people seem forever to lack a sense of body position and coordination; in others, the ability to move with grace and to anticipate the moves of others is a distinct talent. It does not reduce to words, nor to sounds, nor to smells.

While this has been the subject of endless challenges and debates among many in brain science, it is now clear that there are important divisions in the brain. Both hemispheres of the human cerebral cortex also seem to have a special concentration of talents, at least in most people. These talents include the functions of locating and identifying.

Knowing space, for example, is quite important to us. For some people, the task of moving a large sofa around a corner into a small room is a vexing problem, while for others it requires no effort at all. Other spatial abilities, as we have already mentioned, come into play in producing or appreciating sculpture as well as in carpentry and architecture.

An allied talent is the ability to *know place,* to understand where one is and how to retrace the route along which one has traveled. Put people with "place talents" in a new city, and they immediately know how to get to the museums. Others cannot tell their left from their right or identify where north and west are.

The talent to *know faces* is something that most of us have. We seem to be able to remember a face but not necessarily a name, as the cliché has it, because these are different abilities, lodged in different parts of the brain. It is important to know whether one has seen someone before and to be able to decipher the nonverbal communication offered by faces. This ability is innate; it appears early in a child's development with almost no prodding. It depends on some extremely complex circuitry in the parietal lobes. Think of the enormous number of people you can recognize. Brain damage, especially in the parietal lobes, can cause one to lose this ability to recognize faces (a disorder called "prosopagnosia").

A remarkable talent is *calculating,* which we do continuously, not just when we're doing schoolwork or balancing the checkbook. We calculate the movement of objects, our own movements, the weight and brightness of the world, and the effort needed to do something as well as the gains that are likely. Elaborated greatly, this talent becomes a gift for formal mathematics. It is independent of verbal fluency or even logic. Mathematics seems to have a stronger spatial component and less of a verbal one than most people think.

Talking seems to be the function closest to the conventional conception of intelligence, and two separate areas of the left hemisphere control the understanding of words and their production. With some individuals, damage to one or the other of these areas produces quite different kinds of aphasia (loss of language). For example, the first area of the brain to be identified with a talent was "Broca's Area" in the left hemisphere, where damage can destroy the fluency of speech but not the meaning. A person with damage in this area simply no longer has the ability to select the words to express what is "on his or her mind."

Decoding meaning is a separate talent from talking, and it also depends on the interpretations and inferences of the knowledge centers in the brain. *Reading* and *writing* are more highly developed and artificial talents.

There are at least two separate general-knowledge talents and probably more. One, concerned with *processing fine details,* uses the left hemisphere; another, concerned with *connecting observations into a whole,* uses the right. The processing of details involved in logical analysis seems to be independent of the talents of talking and of calculating. This ability to reason, to make critical inferences, can be destroyed by brain damage or stroke, although it clearly is not as organized an area as is the ability to string words together.

There is also an *intuiting* faculty; this is the capacity to determine how the disconnected pieces of a puzzle, either literal or metaphorical, fit together and how elements such as individual unconnected line lengths can come together to make a square. Many people seem to know immediately how to pick the right person, how to find the way out of the woods, or even how to buy the right house at the right time. This is the talent of the artist and the money manager, not the art dealer and the accountant.

Finally, all these pieces get assembled by the organizing center, the locus of the talents for *organizing, inferring, interpreting,* and *controlling.* Here, probably, is where we assemble many of the observations, inferences, and calculations we make about ourselves. Damage to certain parts of this frontal area can result in the inability to carry out plans and to structure the normal routines of daily life. But in some cases, damage to this area even interferes with a person's ability to know on a long-term basis "who" he or she is.

As one might guess from our discussion of deliberation-liberation, a person with frontal deficits or damage may well be able to carry out complex activities almost as normal, but not know why he or she is doing them—why bills are being paid, why a set of people are gathered together for a birthday party, and the like. Remember the French frontal patients Pierre and

Marie who both couldn't behave appropriately in the doctor's office or at a party, and would simply select routines of action that didn't fit.

This self-governing talent probably appeared in humans at about the same time as they developed the ability to plan, to infer, and to abstract information. It became elaborated late in evolution, probably during the emergence of modern man, which is the period of rapid cortical growth that has taken place over the past four million years.

I believe that most of our talents are highly heritable, and psychologist Auke Tellegen, mentioned earlier, seems to provide the most important evidence for the constancy of these different pieces of the puzzle.

Most theories, as we've seen, give great weight to experiences, and we've found that family, for instance, makes little difference at all. Tellegen and his colleagues studied 350 pairs of twins, some raised together, some raised apart. If we compare those raised separately and together, we can get a better view of the effects of heredity. The study found that the twins reared apart were strikingly similar in such areas as how much leadership they displayed, how much achievement they strove for, how intimate they wished to be, and even how "traditional" they were—that is, how closely they would follow the practices that they learned in their youth. In fact, in many cases, the twins reared apart were no less similar than twins reared together. Of course, some twins living together try to be as different as possible, which may affect this comparison somewhat.

Still, these individuals either sought high achievement or didn't care much about what they did, followed authority or not, chose to become intimate with others or stayed aloof—and all these traits seemed to develop without much regard for the life circumstances of the twins. This can tell us two things: these pieces are important aspects of our individuality, and they seem to be independent of experience.

The Self

What we call "the self" is actually just one of the many modules of the mind, independent of the rest, ignorant of what is going on, and must calculate its own conclusions, rightly or wrongly, about the person. We do not have special or direct access to what is going on inside ourselves; often we guess, infer, or calculate it. We do not have the same information about others that we have about ourselves, as our access is both special and limited. On the one hand, we have great and extensive experience of ourselves! For the governing center is always at work while we think, sleep, and act either well or badly. The "self" has access to information about difficulties and extenuating circumstances that it does not possess about others.

We may say, "My mind's made up about this." It seems reasonable that we should know our own minds, and we do, certainly better than we know others'. But we don't know our minds directly or very well, with any more ease or precision than we know how our pancreas is functioning. "Know thyself" is probably more difficult than even Plato imagined.

But the self does have a special place. It contributes most to the top level of the mind where the controlling functions of consciousness occur. Our ordinary speech comes close to an accurate description here, as we speak of self-consciousness, self-understanding, and self-observation as important talents or as disabling factors in a person's makeup.

But the self, although possessing a privileged place in the mind, is more isolated than we might have imagined. It is just another independent talent, located in a specific portion of the brain. It has less special access to other equally important parts of the brain than we think. All a person's different talents and abilities, then, can operate independently and be combined into larger units, just as various members of a team may get called onto a football field.

For example, both spatial and logical abilities are needed to run an architecture business. The emotional talents and the movement ones may combine in expressive dance. The protective aspects of the emotions and our logical capacities may join to form paranoia. One can think of hundreds of likely combinations of these independent pieces of the puzzle. The lack of a talent may be crucial, since, as we've seen, underdevelopment of some emotional reactions may contribute to antisocial behavior, even criminality. Thus, talents are important pieces of the puzzle of the self.

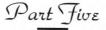
Part Five

Completing Ourselves: Going Beyond Our Inheritance

Of Monkey Brains, Fish Hierarchy, Tame and Wild Cats, Missing Limbs, and the Amazing Possibility of Growth in the Brain

Human beings are not born once and for all on the day their mothers give birth to them. . . . Life obliges them over and over again to give birth to themselves.

GABRIEL GARCIA MARQUEZ

We've traveled a long way in this short book from the place where we described human beings as an "unfinished animal" whose development is completed in the world. Since then we've looked at how temperament, family, race, sex, and brain differences form the roots of our individuality. As you have read about each one, you may have felt more and more as Tess did—that your life is fixed in its course, perhaps predestined entirely. However, we're never boxed in completely.

How much can we change our nature? While there isn't a definitive answer, since most of the research is incomplete and different aspects of ourselves are capable of different rates of change at different times, still we aren't dead yet, and therefore we're not completely fixed by our nature. We can both change it a bit and adapt our lives to suit it.

Experiences, anytime in life, physically change the brain

I've tried to show that we need to analyze the human personality and know ourselves in a new way, one based on our physiology rather than on ideology. Knowing about how our physiology disposes us toward life may provide us with a way to enact real change that is in line with our character, rather than in line with some artificial or arbitrary system. The brain and the nervous system are not immutable; they grow and change with life experiences. Thus, we can take an active role in changing our own brain processes and improve the way we manage ourselves.

Life experiences play a larger role in the brain development of human beings than in that of any other animal. Until recently, physiologists and psychologists supposed that neurons begin to make connections at birth and that these connections increase with age and experience. In fact, the opposite is the case. There are many more connections in the brain of an infant than in a young adult, and a young adult has still more than does an elderly adult.

Development seems to be a matter of "pruning" the original connections rather than of making new ones. In the third trimester of pregnancy (six to nine months), a human baby has about 2.5 million cells behind its retina that carry processed visual information to the brain. An adult has 1.25 million cells with which to analyze that information. Just as we might prune a fruit tree, cell death is the way in which our individuality is initially sculpted out of the wealth of our inheritance.

The brain is special, protected tissue, and it is difficult to carry out the relevant brain studies on human beings, but studies comparing cats' brains find a loss of volume of at least a third during development. Unused connections wither and die, and new connections become possible. Cell death may also be one way in which rapid adaptation occurs. For instance, a wild cat retains much more color vision than does a tame cat. Both the wild cat and the domestic are conceived with the same number of brain cells, but in each species different cells disappear just before birth. This difference has evolved, presumably, because wild cats need to identify threats and sources of food; thus, their brains retain more of the cells that help analyze the complexity of the world.

My own old cat has learned that she needs only to sit at her dish and look pathetic for a can of Friskies to be opened. As the environment of house cats is much more predictable—living amid cat food, heating and cooling systems, and the like—these cats have lost 30 to 50 percent of the brain cells that the wild cat still develops. I am sure that a similar devolution has occurred in humans, too, but there are no studies on this as yet.

Similarly, each human being begins life with the ability to speak any language on earth and countless others long disappeared and not yet invented. Our exposure to local environment early in life lops off everything but the language(s) of our own communities. In the first months of life, a baby utters almost every sound of every known language; later on the individual loses the ability to make sounds that are not in the language he or she has learned to speak. There is thus a universe of potential sound patterns available to us at birth, but we learn only a few of them. Then, once learned, new connections between the existing cells get made as we make new sentences, learn new facts, and develop.

More than other animals, human beings mature biologically outside the womb. The "finishing process" begins early: children differ at birth and parents respond to it, creating radically different worlds for them. Differences in nutrition, in how much parents talk to the baby, and in one's position in one's family can produce significant differences in personality, especially when one's ethnic group has its own specific practices.

Small differences in one's early environment can make very large differences later on. Speaking one's indigenous language early and often and experiencing a high level of sound and light stimulation set the brain on a fast track, while being bound up or bound to the mother, as are Navajo babies, can be the root of a placid detached person.

There are many other ways in which one's early environment has an impact on brain development. Radically deprived children, for example, grow more slowly and can become mentally retarded. The longer children are prevented from learning a language in the early years of their lives, the harder it is for them ever to learn to speak. However, children can also *recover* from deprivation to a remarkable extent. One group of children in a particularly bad orphanage was given almost no stimulation; they lay on their backs all day in bare cribs that stood in bare rooms. They were touched only when their diapers were changed. At the age of one year, their development was about that of a six-month-old. Some of these babies were later adopted, and scientists compared their development with that of the children still left in the orphanage. Those in the orphanage remained retarded, but those who were adopted caught up with other children in many aspects of development. This and many other studies show that we are capable of overcoming many early deprivations *if later experience compensates.*

The brain may be set up at birth to do a myriad of different things, but we only get around to doing a few of them, and so our capacities diminish. Thus, out of a specific genetic heritage, experience sculpts a unique individual.

Cultivating the Brain

One of the most hopeful findings in neuroscience is that how one uses one's brain, even as an adult, has an enormous effect on its structure, even down to the workings of the neurons. I think it's important to take a close and semitechnical look at this evidence.

Human beings, like many other animals, start life with uncultivated brains. The ability of the brain to change its structure, which is called plasticity, is greatest close to the time of birth, when one is open to almost infinite possibilities. The branches of nerves connected to the sense organs, eyes, ears, and skin sensors spread throughout the cortex, the outer surface of the brain where the signals are processed. Certain destinations are preset; the eyes always connect to the visual cortex at the back of the brain.

But it is only through continuous exercise, effort, and stimulation that the highly specialized areas of the cortex of the adult brain develop to their full extent. In the adult visual cortex, there are modules of cells called ocular dominance columns. The cells in one set of columns respond only to input from the nerves of the left eye; the cells in the other set respond only to input from the right eye. These columns alternate along part of the visual cortex. But at birth, there is no such pattern; all the neurons in that area of the brain respond equally to visual stimulation from either eye. This is not simply a matter of incomplete or immature development that the passage of time in the individual animal's life will automatically rectify.

If the visual cortex neurons receive no input, no dominance columns will emerge. If all of the neurons receive the exact same input (which has been tested through artificial stimulation of the optic nerves), still no columns appear. The columns only develop if the animal has normal visual experience of the world—that is, if the right and left eyes see slightly different scenes.

What an eye sees also changes which groups of neurons are turned on by different sources of stimulation. At the start of the brain's life, any visual input causes widespread activity in the visual cortex. But with time, visual experience organizes the cortex into areas specialized for lines, movement, light, and dark.

It happens this way: neurons that are active at the same time become joined. So neurons connected to the left eye, in firing together often, become strongly joined to each other, and they lose many of their connections to neurons from the right eye, which are less synchronized with them. Carla Shatz, a neurobiologist at the University of California, Berkeley, summarized this process of "pruning" neuron connections in this way: "Cells that fire together wire together."

How does this happen? How can experience change neurons? Neurons, which are the basic building blocks of the brain and nervous system, transmit information from one part of the brain or body to another by passing electrical signals along their lengths and by sending chemical messages to each other at their ends. A junction between the end of one neuron and the beginning of another is called a synapse, and this is where the chemical exchange between neurons takes place.

The continuing plasticity of the brain also derives from its far-reaching network of neuronal interconnections. Experience changes the brain by re- or deactivating the connections between neurons. During late childhood, the maturing brain reduces its total number of connections in the cortex. Clear synaptic pruning occurs. If one counts synapses (in post-mortem brain studies) one finds fewer synapses in older brains. Through magnetic resonance imagings (MRIs) one finds that the cortex *actually shrinks* between the ages of five and fifteen.

For experience to alter the brain it must alter the neurons. Neurons do not multiply; we are born with a certain number and lose many along the way in life. However, it is not the number of neurons but their pattern of connection that is altered by experience. Neurons that are active at the same time will have strong connections to each other—connections made at synapses. This may happen through chemical messages that stimulate the growth of more synapses between neurons, or by causing the extension of more branches from a neuron to permit more connections with other neurons. Conversely, connections between neurons that are not simultaneously active become sparser and weaker.

Some of the evidence comes from as far away as rats' brains, monkeys' paws, and fish dominance. Marion Diamond has shown that an animal's environment can change the shape of its brain. In a series of experiments rats were given "enriched" living quarters (twelve rats in a big cage with lots of toys that were changed daily); these rats ended up with thicker cortexes and more neural branches than rats raised in "impoverished" environments, where they were kept alone or with two others in boring cages with no toys.

Differences in cortical thickness were even discovered between rats that had only been separated into enriched and impoverished environments for four days. And these changes happened in mature rats as well as in young, developing ones. There is strong evidence that the world around us affects our growth through our senses. Thus, the rats' enriched environments gave them a larger array of sensory experiences, made possible more variations in behavior, and probably also posed more unique problems to be solved than the impoverished environments.

Introductory textbooks display an illustration of the sensory areas of the brain with a grotesque "homunculus" laid across it. This figure, with enormous lips and fingers and a relatively tiny back and trunk, represents the amount of brain cortex devoted to tactile sensations from these parts of the skin surface. It was once thought that the brain's "body image" was an inherited feature in which all details were set, but the discovery of a wide array of innate neuronal connections that are then pruned by experience has diminished the usefulness of the "hard-wiring" theory. And the reprogramming of cells can happen quickly.

For example, one month after losing an arm in an accident, a person can feel the limb, as the brain "fills in" the map of the body with stimulation from other areas. The cheek and the jaw, for instance, are close to the arm on the brain's map of the body, so stimulation of the cheek may rekindle the feeling of the lost arm.

Michael Merzenich, William Jenkins, Gregg Recanzone, and others at the University of California, San Francisco, have been uncovering fascinating details on how sensory experience affects brains. Merzenich and his colleagues demonstrated that the brain's body maps are changeable with use, even in adult mammals. If a given area of the skin is stimulated repeatedly, more of the cortex will respond to touch on that part of the skin, and that skin area will be represented in finer detail by the brain.

This finding comes from an experiment in which monkeys were taught that they could earn a tasty treat by touching their middle finger with just the right pressure to the edge of a moving grooved wheel. The monkey needed to sense that he or she was holding the right finger with the right pressure in the right place, and the part of the finger that gave the monkey this sensation gained an expanded "map area" in the animal's sensory cortex. Representations of other hand and finger areas rearranged to accommodate the new finger map. The scientists determined the layout of the brain's body map by measuring which cells fired electrical impulses when specific areas of skin were touched.

Other experiments showed that the brain's hand map would change to suit alterations in the input from the skin on the hand. When two fingers were surgically attached so that they always moved together and touched the same things, they developed a fused, single map in the brain, where there had once been a separate map for each of the fingers.

If the researchers relocated a segment of a monkey's hand skin to another part of the hand without disconnecting any nerves, the moved skin's brain map representation would also move in the brain so that it was next to the brain map areas of its new neighboring skin sections. Skin representations line up in the brain based on how frequently the activity from their neurons correspond in time. Two skin patches next to each other are likely to be stimulated at the same time more often than two that are far apart. Thus, the former two patches' maps will be adjacent in the brain, and the latter two maps will be separate.

The plasticity of the brain's representations of the body are essential to recovery from certain kinds of brain damage. If the part of a monkey's brain that responds to a hand area is damaged, nearby parts of the brain pick up the job of processing the information from the hand.

How much malleability is there in the layout of the brain? It has been a common assumption that the layout of specialized areas in one species would be different from the map of another species of animal, just as their actual physical body plans differ.

However, Merzenich found that the variation in brain maps of hands between individuals of one species was greater than the variation found on average between different species of monkey. All monkeys have "hands." But every individual monkey has had a unique lifetime of experience, reflected in differences in the way it has used its hands and therefore in its brain's hand maps. This individual difference in experience creates a greater difference in the monkey's brains than do the genetic differences between the species.

An intriguing possibility raised by Merzenich is that assignments of cortical brain areas are not, as our developmental neurobiologists have thought, inherited genetically. Perhaps the layout of the brain's map of sensation comes entirely from the experiences provided by the senses! A monkey may have inherited the genes for a tail; however, if the monkey's brain never receives any sensory information from the tail, it will never develop a representation for a tail.

The brain areas responsible for movements are similarly affected by experience: the motor areas of the preferred hand have more complex layouts in the brain than those for the nonpreferred hand. Consider, says Merzenich, writer's cramp, a condition in which people can no longer write because their hands seize into rigid postures as soon as they pick up a pen. This affliction reached a peak in the Victorian era, which one pair of researchers attributes to "the success of the British Empire, the enormous office staff required to run it, and the difficulties of manipulating the quill pen." By spending endless hours inscribing tiny numbers in ledgers and filling out innumerable forms—in other words, by using their dominant hand in the same way over and over so that the brain received only the same set of stimuli from that hand—these office clerks may have trained all flexibility out of their brains' ability to control their hands while writing; eventually, they were left with little but an overwhelming impulse to grip the pen. So writer's cramp probably was not just simple muscle fatigue but actually represented a change in the brain's body map brought about by experience.

Social Factors in the Development of the Neuronal System

Social factors also change the brain, even in fish. Neurophysiologists Mark Davis and Russ Fernald discovered that a social factor was a prime consideration in the development of a neuronal system in a species of fish. The adult male African cichlid is territorial and vicious to competing adult males. The researchers found that young male cichlids ordinarily do not reach sexual maturity for about two years, but they would mature in three months if there were no adult males in the vicinity.

The restraint on the sexual development of males was caused by the suppression of the growth of the neurons in the brain responsible for producing the hormones needed to stimulate sexual development. The young fish's senses were picking up some kind of information from the older males' presence that prevented a certain set of neurons in their brains from growing.

What can fish teach us about ourselves? The existence of such a social mechanism regulating brain structural growth hints that similar events could be possible in other species, although there is no evidence of this. We share some basic genetic inheritance with fish; like us, they are vertebrates (creatures with backbones) and have complex central and peripheral nervous systems.

Shaping Ourselves by Shaping Our Brains

So we come into the world with the basic human inheritance. But in order to become individuals, we must have human experience. Our environment and actions shape our brains' internal connections, the way we process information from the senses, and even what aspects of the world we are able to perceive. The fundamentals of our perceptual abilities, such as whether we see out of both eyes, are shaped in the first few years of life. For the rest of our lives, however, our brains change constantly, reflecting our life situations, the environment around us, and the activities we choose to pursue. Given the knowledge that we are what we do, we can use our extraordinary human capacity for reason and forethought to select how we want to program our own brains.

One way in which to take advantage of the effect of experience on the brain is through rehabilitation. Early malnutrition results in the underdevelopment of the brain, but this can be reversed in rats by providing them with a stimulating environment. Stroke victims can, over time, recover functions lost due to brain damage, since other brain areas will take over the functions once carried out by the damaged areas. If we can discover how training alters our brain maps, then we might be able to develop therapy programs that would accelerate the recovery of lost abilities. And those of us with normal, healthy brains could learn how to enhance capacities that would serve us in the complex modern world.

Cultural Differences in Response to Pain

*J*ust how far can we go to change ourselves? The evidence is difficult to assemble. We know from many anecdotes that people from different cultures have radically different responses to the world, including pain.

Mark Zborowski interviewed a number of hospital patients in New York City and found that people from different cultures experienced their pain differently. "An old American Protestant talked about pain this way, 'I don't cry—I want to take my pain like a man—I want to be a real man and not tell my pain.' 'I don't scream or cry, just sit there and take it. I don't fight, just sit there. What can you do? No use hollering or fighting it.'"

Jewish patients, on the other hand, were not quite the same. "Yesterday it hit me like hell. I was crying like a baby so the nurse came in. I don't know what I would have done if she hadn't helped me." "I cried once when I was in severe pain, it was a helpless feeling. More like tears came to my eyes in the light, I felt so helpless."

Irish Americans were similar to Protestants. "Oh, no, I wouldn't complain. I'd just wait until it went away, that's all. I'm not that bad about it." Italian patients were more expressive: "No, no, no, you can't hide it. It's too tough. Yeah, you can't hide it. You know you've got it because you've got to moan or scream or do something. Oh, when the pain came, I . . . I . . . I mean I just can't stand the pain, it brings tears to my eyes."

Here is a description by British physician P. E. Brown of tonsillectomies in China, showing, at the very least, some slight cultural differences from our own:

> While visiting a children's hospital, we saw a queue of smiling five-year-olds standing outside the room where tonsillectomies were being carried out in rapid succession. The leading child was given a quick anesthetic spray of the throat by a nurse a few minutes before walking into the theater unaccompanied. Each youngster in turn climbed on the table, lay back smiling at the surgeon, opened his mouth wide, and had his tonsils dissected out in the extraordinary time of less than a minute. The only instruments he used were dissecting scissors and forceps. The child left the table and walked into the recovery room, spitting blood into a gauze swab. A bucket of water at the surgeon's feet containing thirty-four tonsils of all sizes was proof of a morning's work.

There have been physiological studies of different people's responses to pain. In one experiment, women volunteers were encouraged to submit to stronger and stronger electric shocks until they found it uncomfortable to continue. The results of the experiment were that women from Italian backgrounds reported discomfort at much lower intensities than did women from Irish and Protestant backgrounds. The Protestant women were much more relaxed while they were receiving the shocks than were the other women. It was perhaps the matter-of-fact attitude of this group toward pain that helped them achieve this physiological reaction. The Irish women, however, did not show a relaxed physiological reaction; they were apparently not so adaptive.

In another study, researchers recruited Jewish and Christian college students and exposed them to pain from a blood pressure cuff. Jewish and Christian participants significantly increased their pain tolerance when they were told beforehand that their religious group was thought to be inferior in its tolerance for pain.

To see in detail how extreme are the changes that can occur in human brains, we need to consider extraordinary events. It is impossible to measure what might go on deep inside the brain of a middle-aged person when he or she learns the guitar. We also can't duplicate in the laboratory the effects of the extremes of war on individuals. Yet changes in the brain provoked by life experiences can sometimes happen quite rapidly, with effects as dramatic as might be expected from a physical blow to the head.

Combat veterans, hostages, and victims of rape, child abuse, assault, or natural disasters frequently suffer long-lasting symptoms, referred to as posttraumatic stress disorder (PTSD).

Posttraumatic Stress Disorder

*P*eople with PTSD are hyperreactive to the world around them. Minor startling events can trigger reexperiences of the trauma, such as hallucinations of being back in the combat zone. Victims frequently explode in aggressive outbursts and cannot keep thoughts of danger out of their minds. They have recurring nightmares. PTSD sufferers retreat from social and emotional commitments, become irresponsible at work, show little emotional expression outside of outbursts, may find themselves in legal troubles, and experience little life pleasure. These difficulties can last for decades. One Vietnam veteran, quoted in the 1985 report of a study by Bessel van der Kolk and colleagues, described his state:

> After a certain moment you just keep running the 100-yard dash. I spend all my energy on holding it back. I have to isolate myself to keep myself from exploding. It all comes back all the time. The nightmares come two, three times a week for a while. . . . You can never get angry, because there is no way of controlling it. You can never feel just a little bit. It is all or nothing. I am constantly and totally preoccupied with not getting out of control.

PTSD patients live in a constant state of preparedness to defend themselves against the danger that originally caused the problem. For this lasting damage to occur, a person must experience a truly terrifying event with the sense of having no control over it. Scientists studying anxiety disorders have induced in laboratory animals a condition similar to PTSD by subjecting them to painful shocks from which they cannot escape. Drugs that deplete certain brain messenger chemicals produce animal behaviors like those evoked by the inescapable shocks.

Clues like this have led researchers to look for unusual features in the brain chemistry of people with PTSD. The chemicals the brain uses to initiate the "fight-or-flight" response to danger are chronically present at high levels in PTSD patients. One of these chemicals, norepinephrine, has far-ranging influences: it diminishes the ability to sleep, increases alertness, elevates heart rate and blood pressure, promotes the release of hormones that mediate the body-wide response to stress, and possibly causes "flashbacks" and nightmares duplicating the traumatic events.

Some parts of the brain and body adapt to the high levels of hormones by reducing sensitivity to them, while others do not, causing disorder in the nervous system, tipping it toward constant anxiety and overreaction. The outpouring of these chemicals may lead to their absence in some parts of the brain following periods of anxiety, and this absence can lead to such behavioral symptoms as low emotional reactivity, shaky hands, jerky movement, exaggerated startle responses, and speaking difficulties.

Another brain system linked to stress and disrupted in PTSD is the endogenous opiate pain-reducing circuit. Intense fear or pain releases floods of substances, including opiates, in the brain and body to reduce unpleasant sensations, presumably to permit the person or animal to function and fight in order to escape harm. One study found that combat veterans with PTSD had reduced sensitivity to pain after they watched a segment of the movie *Platoon* (about the Vietnam war), which simulated combat. The PTSD patients reported that viewing the film was extremely unpleasant. Participants in this study who did not have PTSD found the scene distressing but showed no subsequent increase in their pain thresholds. The pain sensitivity of those with PTSD was reduced as much as if they had received an injection of eight milligrams of morphine.

Essentially, the combat veterans with PTSD responded to the clip as if they were in a life-threatening situation. PTSD researcher Bessel van der Kolk suggested that because PTSD sufferers pour so much natural pain-killer into their systems at so little provocation, the victims become addicted to their own internal narcotics. There's a similarity between the systems of opiate (such as heroin) withdrawal and PTSD; both are characterized by anxiety, irritability, unpredictable rage, insomnia, and hyperalertness. Also, the opioid system in the brain is closely linked to the norepinephrine (adrenaline) system, both of which participate in responding to danger. These two systems, disordered in PTSD, probably act together to produce the unpleasant symptoms.

Some people exposed to catastrophes spend the rest of their lives seeking out further traumatic events, bringing themselves into emergency situations or taking up dangerous careers as soldiers, firefighters, or police officers. These people may be addicted to the flow of internal opiates, requiring frequent fear to prevent the occurrence of withdrawal symptoms. They may need to seek continuous excitement through horror movies, dangerous sports like white-water rafting, or fast driving. These sensation seekers need the stimulation required to produce their own internal opiates, not the **RAS** stimulation sought by extroverts.

These changes in the brains of those exposed to catastrophes can happen through a process known as neural kindling, which has been studied in rats. Electrical stimulation of the amygdala of rats eventually leads to a permanent "heating up" of the responsiveness. If one gives a rat thirty to sixty days of daily one-second repeated stimulation bursts, the animal begins to have spontaneous convulsions that emanate from the limbic system even after the electrical stimulation has ceased. If inhibited children have a more excitable circuit leading from their amygdala to the hypothalamus, a frightening environmental event might function as a similar kindling stimulus. The trauma that causes posttraumatic stress disorder may also have a kindling effect in the brain, ensuring that future activities will pass along an already "warm" pathway. This is what may lead **PTSD** sufferers to be irritable and extrasensitive to glitches in the world.

PTSD shows that if an experience is intense enough, it can change the way the brain works even in adulthood. At the time of World War I, some believed postcombat trauma symptoms to be "shell shock," caused by physical concussion to the brain. We now know that the actual effect is on the neurons of the brain, but it has an equally overwhelming impact on the life of the trauma survivors, affecting almost every aspect of their ability to function in human society. It is not easy for these people to recover normal functions because of the widespread unbalancing of their nervous systems, which have become programmed to deal only with terrible threats. Behavior therapy and treatment with drugs that restore balance to brain chemicals are now being developed and becoming available to help **PTSD** patients live normal, productive lives.

Our brains are constantly in flux, adapting to serve our lives. Of course, changes in adulthood are not usually as dramatic as those in childhood, when we learn language and the ways of our local world, but change is possible at any time through the selection and deselection of neural pathways. It isn't that one has to have an experience as dramatic as a major trauma in order to change; it's simply that right now these dramatic changes are easier to study.

There's no point in life at which we can't grow and develop, even if that growth is related to one of the roots of the self. We can't change much about how we amplify the world nor much of our basic mood *predispositions,* but we can change our *experienced* mood by doing things that make us happy and concentrating on optimistic interpretations.

I know this sounds a little simplistic, yet there is a lot of research that backs it up: even silently repeating things like "Every day in every way I am getting better and better" does have long-lasting results, as does learning to interpret the events of our life in a more positive manner, as does cognitive therapy. Optimists live longer, are freer from disease, and recover from surgery faster. Is this just innate? No, for people who obtain training to become more optimistic also increase their immunity to disease! This is why taking up new challenges throughout life is most often associated with increased health; it also indicates that if we make minor changes, the major changes in life will also be possible. In the final chapter, we'll briefly discuss some of the ways in which we can manage change, taking into account what we now know about our basic nature.

On Human Nature and Individual Human Nature

Changes Large and Small

*I*n some of my previous books, I've written about the ever-changing separated nature of the self. I devoted one book to how the mind has different reactions to handle different situations. This book considers the question of the origins of such variety: how each individual develops so differently. As anybody knows, individual human beings have different mental organizations, temperaments, and predilections from one another.

A few of the main dimensions, I believe, derive from archaic brain systems. They are continua of low and high gain, deliberation-liberation, and approach-withdrawal. These three overarching systems compose the roots of our actions—whether we're quick to boil over or to smile, whether we frantically search the world for fun or quietly stay inside ourselves, whether we plan our lives out or take things one moment at a time. But other completely independent factors enter in, such as our hemisphere organization as revealed in our handedness, the profound sex differences, and the miscellany of our talents. With all this complexity, no one is ever exactly like anyone else.

The fact of individuality is basic to our lives. Learning to tell people apart and understanding our own unique potential are central to us. Thus, one would have thought that psychological science would begin there. However, this analysis is more of a departure than it ought to be, since American psychology and other associated disciplines such as neurobiology and psychiatry have

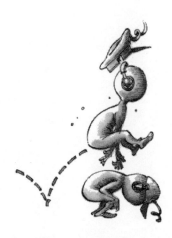

Each of us goes beyond
our inheritance

195

not focused much on individuality; they have concentrated instead on the regularities in human thought and action. Instead of looking at *individual* brains, these scientists have tried to discover how *"the"* brain works.

Psychologists, especially, have given precedence to the general case rather than the individual. Instead of attempting to understand the unique logic of any one individual's decision making, they look for the logic in the general rules for making decisions. And the same is true of creativity, the regulation of behavior, and the rest.

It's ironic that American culture is one that so prizes individual effort in sports, in science, in business (we all know the names Iacocca and Trump, and the heads of many corporations, but we don't know who is or who ever was the head of Nikon or Mitsubishi, and neither do the Japanese) but does not have much of a tradition for discovering the fundamental ways in which individuals differ from one another. This lack of an idea of our variability also gives us a weird and too-limited view of what normality is. In America, we are very quick to decide that a person has some serious disturbance, while such judgments are not so common in other cultures, notably in England, where there is much more of a tradition of respecting large individual variation.

We should consider ourselves differently to take into account "human nature." A first step is to look at the complex of factors I described in Chapter Three using Don Brown's description of the "Universal People." While each of us certainly inherits the basis for human nature, and the regularities of life on earth bring the rest of these characteristics out (the common need for respiration, for food, for reproduction; common experiences like seeing the moon and encountering gravity), we also inherit an individual human nature. In this book, I've made a stab at describing the overarching dimensions of individuality as well as the miscellany of other factors that make us so complex.

If we were to take to heart some of this information, our society might well make changes in several specific areas. First, if the brain is constantly changing after birth and adapts to its locale most radically early in life, then the major strategy for removing inequality should focus on early intervention. While adult affirmative action programs may be necessary now to rectify the longstanding effects of discrimination, the most truly affirmative action would be the earliest action.

If one group of people, whether defined by skin color, ethnicity, or some other characteristic, has a lower average birth weight and disadvantageous early learning experiences, then a program that intervenes at the moment of conception (at the latest) would make the biggest difference in changing head size, birth weight, and the chances of future illness. For instance, given the understanding that an intact nervous system is essential, one would look upon massive immunizations and prenatal interventions as having perhaps the biggest payoff. Children who are challenged with deficiencies cannot develop as they might.

If we looked aright at our society's priorities, differences we currently interpret as racial might well disappear. My hope is that our society will equalize the opportunities given to people of different skin colors so that we can stop arguing about the influence of race on IQ.

In arenas that range from chess to sports to business, sex differences are diminishing, but unlike race differences, some of these central differences will never disappear completely, even as they become less important due to reproductive and social freedom. The differences between males and females are not skin deep in all areas, especially in reproductive choices and some spatial functions, and we shouldn't be beholden to false political agendas about the identicalness of the sexes.

There are more local lessons, too. Parents might well note that disparities in how they treat their different children affect the children's development. If we want to avoid many of the resentments common among our different offspring, we should minimize these differences in treatment as much as possible. But to aim to feel the same about all our children, as well as to treat them similarly, would be asking more than is humanly possible. I simply suggest that knowing the effects of preferential treatment might help parents understand some of the reasons that their children behave as they do.

Individual Human Nature

Our individual human nature is a pastiche of independent factors. Whether we are high gain and need little outside stimulation or low gain and need much has nothing to do with whether we are female or left-handed or secondborn. But once we are set along a particular route, we cannot obliterate our past. If you are born female, you will always be female, and so it is with the dimensions of temperament and handedness. When psychologists and other theorists have tried to describe a personality as a whole, too often they have tried to rely on a single descriptor such as "egocentric" or "mesomorphic." In a sense, this idea that each person has a single "self" has obscured our essential variety.

The primary question is which descriptors, which parts of the self, are significant. One person might find it helpful to be described as an Aquarius or as an oral person with strong libidinal tendencies. You might say that you are an antisocial personality with a paranoid tendency, or you might call yourself an endomorph. You might consider yourself abused and in recovery. For me, as my favorite Yogi, Berra, might have said, these are all "*déjà lu* all over again.*" I am not convinced that these simplistic forays into describing the personality really help us understand anything that we don't know and haven't read already.

If we are so different from one another and also contain inside ourselves such independent determinants of how to act, from our sex to our regulatory capabilities, why, then, do we feel that we're consistent and coherent? Sometimes the genesis of one action may be a highly deliberated set of rules; another may come from a sexual prompting; a third may result from our position in our family; and so on.

We *learn* to interpret people and things as constant. The reason that children have such difficulty in getting to know the world is that they have to learn the rules of making things constant; they have to have time to build up their representations. For most of their early years, until they can develop a means of figuring out what is going on inside themselves, they don't even know what—or that—they are thinking.

Simply put, we all subscribe to the illusion that objects, people, and ourselves are constant, when in fact they change all the time. It is a useful illusion; without it, we wouldn't know whom to talk to, or what to talk about, or which door to use. But the system breaks down when we try to understand ourselves, since we are trying to be observers in our own lives. This is especially difficult because we do not have any direct access to our own decisions, although, of course, we believe that we know what we are doing. Since we don't have direct access, we have to make up a self-description, just as we make up a way to categorize other people.

The part of us that is the "self itself" is, in fact, just one component of the brain, located in the frontal lobes. It gathers information together and constructs our idea of ourselves. It's as Kurt Vonnegut said, we have to be careful about who we assume we are, because that is who we become. If we had some kind of direct knowledge of our minds and selves, things would be different. But that is not the animal we are.

How do the "higher" aspects of the self, like generosity, humility, intuition, creativity, and the like, fit into the scheme I've proposed? Why haven't I discussed them? I used *roots* in the title of this book to acknowledge that we are at the beginning of an understanding of individuality; thus, we need to focus on those elements that can be established through studies of physiology, through testing, and through clinical or ordinary observation. Unfortunately, the important human attributes of generosity, intuition, and so on are much more ephemeral from a scientific standpoint, although not from a personal one. Gain, deliberation-liberation, approach-withdrawal—these are my candidates for the roots, not the flowers, of the self.

Looking at roots is a good starting point because the large-scale psychological analyses of commonality of function, brain processes, and judgmental routines conducted over the last hundred years haven't helped us much. These attributes might be somewhat useful in describing human nature but not in explaining an individual human being's nature. Individuals are interested in why they are the way they are, not why everybody is the way he or she is. After all, in describing someone as an "upright hind-leg walker with a family, embedded in a social organization with rules for action," one doesn't feel a lot of excitement.

If the three continua begin to help in understanding ourselves and others, it may be because they describe the characteristics that are most difficult to change—whether we do things cautiously, quietly, with bravado, joyously, and so on. They don't have much to do with the "what" of a life—our goals, careers, and the rest.

We often confuse the "how" with the "what" of a person; we may think, "He was so dedicated to raising money for the poor; how could he be such a sourpuss, or such a sensation seeker, or so unfeeling?" We get surprised all the time. The press never fails to note, in each report of the trial of Sicily's most dreaded godfather, that the don, from Corleone, is shy, quiet, and courtly. We don't expect a don to be high gain; we expect someone more like the extrovert New York Mafia boss John Gotti. They've both got the same "profession," and both are successful. *How* they do their work, however, is different.

In addition, most psychologists and psychiatrists have tried to understand the ordinary mind and self through the unusual. They've done this by looking at what goes wrong in memories, in brain functions, in illusions, in mental disorders, and in what Sigmund Freud called "the psychopathology of everyday life"— that is, in mistakes or slips and their relationship to mind and consciousness.

After a century of this work, it may well be time to reverse the program, to think about disorders as extremes of the norm, studying them as continuous with the normal brain processes. Of course, there have been sound strategic as well as practical reasons for spotlighting disorders. The scientific information available a century ago was very limited and for the most part either ridiculous or plain wrong. Freud and his contemporaries wrote at a time when the nature, psychology, and evolution of the brain were not understood, when there was no tradition of cognitive or neuroscience, and the massive data now available from personality and intellectual testing was not available, let alone codified. When Freud wrote *The Interpretation of Dreams*, the brain was still considered a single mass; even decades later, the discovery of the neuron was heresy.

In such an environment, the accessibility of florid and striking cases of hysteria, depression, catatonia, schizophrenia, amnesia, or autism would seem to offer an immediate analysis of what was going wrong in these people.

However, the progress since then has been slight at best. Another reason for this is the departmental nature of scientific thought. Psychiatry has a different data base, a different set of journals and concerns and internal debates than does psychology, and neurobiology and genetics are further away still. Thus, advances in understanding brain evolution rarely get communicated across disciplinary lines. Work on obsessive-compulsive disorder doesn't influence analysis of cognition. A new understanding of the nature of perception doesn't make it into psychiatric discussion. I believe our future progress depends on a more complete look, involving the brain, self, genes, society, and a model like the continua I propose. My specific continua will surely be superseded by a more comprehensive analysis, but the basic concept may remain. When this happens, we will begin to have a good idea of both human nature and individual human nature.

Where We Can Change

$\mathcal{Y}$ou can't change human nature, true. And to a great extent, you can't change your individual human nature. If you are male, your options for changing your sex are small—not nonexistent but very small. It is the same with handedness, the ability to recognize faces, and language abilities. But there is a bit more to be said about changes when we look at the three dimensions: gain, deliberation-liberation, and approach-withdrawal.

While many of our responses are inherent to us, we can either adapt ourselves to them or try to adapt our world to our nature, an approach different from the normal therapeutic or advisory mentality. Gordon Claridge, whose work is quite important in understanding the basic dimensions of our character, discusses one instance when he was in a therapeutic relationship:

> The possibility of explicitly utilising that fact [temperamental differences] in a treatment situation came to me some years ago when I was involved in the behaviour modification of compulsive gamblers. At the time I was employing an unsatisfactory therapeutic mixture of deconditioning, amateur psychotherapy, and exhortation. Finally, faced with one particularly intractable case, I decided, in desperation, to try a different strategy. The man in question had previously been a fairly successful entrepreneur who had, however, squandered away on the racecourse most of the proceeds from his various business interests. In personality he was like most compulsive gamblers, a risk-taking impulsive, sensation-seeking man—and I told him so. I explained bluntly that there was not very much he could do about his temperament but that he could exploit his disposition to gamble in life by directing it towards more personally (and financially) satisfying ends, such as trying to reconstruct his businesses, before it was too late. Strangely, no one among the many professionals from whom he had sought advice had suggested to him that slant on his problem; yet it

proved very effective as a "cure" for his gambling, turning an otherwise psychologically and domestically destructive tendency into a personally fulfilling and socially acceptable form.

GORDON CLARIDGE, *ORIGINS OF MENTAL ILLNESS*

If we understand that our basic temperament is relatively fixed, we might be able to initiate a different approach to self-management. This is somewhat like knowing the nature of the horse you are riding. You can try some maneuvers with a placid horse that you wouldn't try with a skittish one. Similarly, we need to know ourselves in order to "ride" in the most appropriate way.

Observing the self in this way might well make it easier to make choices about how we organize our lives. If you are the sort of person who needs lots of stimulation and you are getting it by having frequent affairs that upset your partner or by causing disruptions with people at work, you might get the same excitement by taking up a dangerous sport instead. Go kayaking or bungee jumping, or go to horror movies. If you don't recognize that your behavior is all about stimulation, you may get bogged down in irrelevant discussions about freedom or the need for self-expression.

Since we normally move up and down the continua with different circumstances, one good way to effect useful change is to alter the situation you are in. You might think, for example, of changing your work so that the situation is a better match for your temperament. Low-gain people can get some of the stimulation they need if they take jobs in fire departments, emergency medicine, stock trading, and the like. Often people who are low gain but who are also a bit disorganized (and liberated) find that the immediate demands of such situations stimulates them to work in a clear and organized way, even though they may well return to their looser style when the pressure is off.

If you are a blitzed high gainer, on the other hand, you may find yourself stressed out at work when nobody else is. If you can't stand the heat, as Truman said, get out of the kitchen, and as I say, get into the library or into computers or air traffic control.

There are a few areas in which it might be useful to go against our inherent reactions. If you find that you are chronically on the negative side of emotionality, you might recall that in gen-

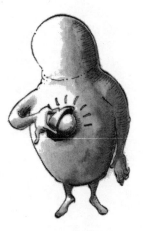

eral, people who have a more positive attitude live longer and stay healthier. You might try to do things that will shift your mood, even if this simply means watching funny videos and the like. Similarly, extroverts are happier than introverts; knowing this, an introvert ought to consider going out more.

There's much misunderstanding when temperamental types mix. A high-gain type in a couple might take the fact that the spouse always wants to go out, doesn't want to sit still and relax at home, as a personal insult. "What's wrong with me? Why doesn't she or he want to be with me at home?" During the early period of a relationship or marriage, we all tend to forget our own nature, and the arousal is enough to keep things harmonious for a while. When that cools, however, we often go back to type. It's important either to understand your partner's individuality and accept it or to realize that any attempt to change them is going to be met with resentment and alter the relationship accordingly.

Finally, some familiar "types" may appear when individuals combine extremes on the three dimensions. A combination of high gain and high negativity would lead to avoidant behavior and shyness, as in the shy and inhibited children studied by Kagan. Low gain and negative emotionality could lead to dangerous sensation seeking. Boris Yeltsin, in his autobiography, said that in his youth, he was constantly getting into scrapes. When he was a child, he and his friends stole some hand grenades to find out how they worked, and he blew up two of his fingers. He bummed rides on freight trains and gambled extensively, once losing all his clothes. Yet individuals who seek out this negative and dangerous stimulation can also find themselves acting as heroes. Yeltsin's greatest moment, at this writing, was surely when he stood on the tanks, risking his life while bravely resisting the Russian coup of 1991. On the other hand, as Bull Meacham in *The Great Santini* said, it's difficult to be a "war hero without a war."

Whether we can use the information presented here to change our individual character and to determine the proper manner of intervention depends, of course, on the adequacy of the analysis. My concept of the roots of the self either works or it doesn't. Let's consider, for example, whether the factors I've presented can help us to describe—admittedly in gross shorthand—an individual human being.

Here's one: female, secondborn with a sister two years older and two younger brothers, parents do not divorce, right-handed, right-eyed, low gain, highly deliberate, positive emotions, has good music talent, good verbal memory, good spatial abilities, and bad place and face talents.

A second: male, left-handed, only child, high gain, anxious, sloppy, disorganized personally, neutral in emotions to slightly negative, stays away from threats, shy, highly intellectual, bad verbal memory, highly creative, myopic, good at recognizing faces, can't remember names.

I guess this all comes down to a question of whether these descriptions, which are based on physiology and testing, are or are not useful in helping us to understand other people and ourselves. While these descriptors certainly don't even begin to exhaust the list of a person's attributes (there is also industriousness, perseverance, competitiveness, hostility, and so on), we would certainly have less trouble recognizing someone so described than if we only "know" them by archetype, sun sign, or stage of development at which they are fixated.

And this is my point: I am making a plea at once for acknowledging the complexity of individuality and at the same time for trying to simplify it by organizing massive amounts of information about the ways in which we differ.

It is possible to "make sense" out of each other by using the continua and the talents, family position, and so on, just as we can do the same with astrology or body types. However, the hope is a bit greater—that we can make a new beginning in studies of individuality to combine the massive evidence provided by personality and intelligence testing, by studies of brain evolution and organization, and by clinical observations—and this combination, in turn, may lead to a more scientifically based view of the roots of the self.

Otherwise, I'd be just as well off waiting, several decades later, for the super-eagle.

Acknowledgments

This book covers a wide territory, from the controversy over eugenics, to studies of the relationship between the family and schizophrenia, to outcomes of psychological testing, studies of handedness, and views of psychiatric disorders. In order to consider the latest work in all of these fields, I have had the benefit of working with many people to whom I would like to show appreciation.

Lynne Levitan did her usual superb job of reviewing complex biological research, while Jerome Burne contributed much on handedness and on temperament, Denise Winn on the family environment, Christina Lepnis on eugenics and cultural relativism, and Pat Williams on case histories. To all of you, many, many thanks.

Many people helped with the inevitable revisions. Seventeen asked to remain anonymous, but I'd like to thank (in reverse alphabetical order) Fred Zlotnick, Pat Williams, David Widdicombe, Brian Taylor, Alan Parker, Evan Neilsen, Lynn Levitan, Christina Lepnis, Linda Garfield, Shane deHaven, and Brent Danninger for their careful readings and Sally Mallam for her rereadings, suggestions on areas that needed further work, and her forbearance during the writing.

Recommended Reading

Whenever one writes a book, there are always some works that one reads that are particularly stimulating as one develops one's ideas. Here are the books that I would highly recommend for further reading.

1. Gordon Claridge, *Origins of Mental Illness: Temperament, Deviance, and Disorder.* New York: Basil Blackwell, 1986.

   This book brings together so many useful points that I have to say that my book would have been impossible without it. Claridge is able to integrate the Eysenck tradition of work with an appreciation of the two hemispheres as well as a lucid discussion of the continuum of mental health, mental states, and illness. I wish I had come upon this book sooner—but I might not have written *Roots* in the same way if I had!

   Gordon Claridge, Ruth Pryor, and Gwen Watkins, *Sounds from the Bell Jar.* London: Macmillan, 1990.

   A superb look at the question of the relationship between psychosis and creativity.

2. Merlin Donald, *Origins of the Modern Mind: Three Stages in the Evolution of Culture and Cognition.* Cambridge, MA: Harvard University Press, 1991.

   An excellent discussion of how the human mind was formed. Brings together cognition as well as social changes—most unusual for a psychologist.

3. Judy Dunn and Robert Plomin, *Separate Lives: Why Siblings Are So Different.* New York: Basic Books, 1990.

   A comprehensive discussion of both of their views on the nature of inheritance and the family. Both Dunn and Plomin conduct research at Pennsylvania State University, which is also home to Patricia Draper, whose work on the relevance of home environment is equally revolutionary.

4. I. I. Gottesman, *Schizophrenia Genesis: The Origins of Madness.* New York: W. H. Freeman, 1991.

   A comprehensive and readable discussion of why schizophrenia befalls certain people, with emphasis on the genetics of the disorder.

5. Ernest Hartmann, *Boundaries in the Mind.* New York: Basic Books, 1992.

An innovative discussion of how the separation of functions is a relevant psychiatric category, perhaps rivaling the older "defense mechanisms" idea. This book offers a related way of describing the deliberation-liberation continuum.

6. Jerome Kagan, *Unstable Ideas: Temperament, Cognition, and Self.* Cambridge, MA: Harvard University Press, 1989.

Describes Kagan's recent research. This book is a little out of date as his most recent work is more important; it is also somewhat discursive, roaming into diverse parts, but it is worth reading.

7. James Q. Wilson and Richard Herrnstein, *Crime and Human Nature.* New York: Simon & Schuster, 1985.

A controversial investigation of criminality from a hereditarian point of view. Badly reviewed when it came out, it contains a wealth of detail in it even for those who do not share the second author's sometimes virulent viewpoint.

Notes

Chapter 2: Coming of Age in Self-Understanding

The early 1900s saw a major division within the discipline of biology, not just between biology and anthropology as was mentioned in the text. Galton's ideas dominated the intellectual climate of that time. The "other side" was represented by T. H. Huxley and E. Ray Lankaster (director of the British Museum of Natural History), both of whom were followers of Darwinian thought.

In *Evolution and Ethics and Other Essays* (1894), Huxley describes "the history of civilization" as the series of stages humans have passed through in "building up an artificial world within the cosmos . . . a process essentially different from that which brought about the evolution of species, in the state of nature." Lankaster focused on the educability of humans versus apes, drawing a distinction between educability, which is a heritable trait, and the results of education, which cannot be inherited and must be *acquired* by an individual. Lankaster used the term *tradition* to mean the results of education; *culture* was the equivalent term for Boas and his colleagues.

Although Boas's academic background was steeped in physics as well as the natural sciences in general, he developed a strong interest in humanistic philosophy while still a student. He was predominantly influenced by a number of men who molded the German Enlightenment: J. G. Herder (who claimed that humans make the world that they inhabit), Schiller (different customs are the agents of divisions among people), and Immanuel Kant (even though humans are a product of nature, they have the ability to make choices and are thus able to shape both themselves and society).

Two other historical figures moved Boas to the cause of cultural determinism. One, Rudolph Virchow, Germany's most famous anthropologist of the time, objected to Darwinian theory once it was applied to humans. He could not support the notion that humans had any phylogenetic ties to other living creatures, and he felt that the combination of evolutionism and a socialist revolution was a dangerous one.

The other figure was Theodor Weitz, another German anthropologist, who believed in the inheritance of physical and mental acquired character. In his *Introduction to Anthropology,* translated in 1863, he even writes of the heritability of battle scars. A champion of the notion that humans are "plastic" and not limited by physical determinism, he went so far as to say that "the shape of the skull is everywhere essentially dependent on mental culture," and he felt that the (apparently) altered body proportions of foreign immigrants had been "directly affected by financial panics."

Mead had a romantic, preconceived picture of life in the South Seas. This was a vision common to most Westerners ever since explorers had visited that part of the world in the late eighteenth century and had returned with glorious descriptions of lush greenery, an idyllic life-style, a balmy climate, the people's libertine ways, and so on.

Mead began her study of the language only after she had arrived in Samoa, and by the time she was fairly well versed in it, she had already completed a great deal of her research. She was never able to master the subtleties of the language.

Samoans themselves have raised the likelihood that Mead's adolescent informants were providing her with some false information. Deliberately misleading people is a game for many Samoans; there is even a word in Samoan for that activity. This game appears to be a kind of playful escape from the many restrictions of daily life, and it seems likely that Mead found herself in such a game.

The teenage girls whom Mead interviewed had, of course, no inkling of the immense influence the anthropologist would have. They were unaware of Darwin and of the "hereditary improvement" proposed by Galton; they had no sense of the importance of the study Mead was conducting and no idea that what they were telling her would end up in published form.

Boas was so enthusiastic about receiving the desired "proof" for cultural determinism that he never had someone else verify Mead's findings by conducting a second investigation. Also, he failed to read up on others' previous accounts of Samoan life. Such ethnographic literature was easily accessible and would have shown Mead's conclusions to be markedly different from past observations of Samoan behavior.

In pagan Samoa, virginity among girls had been valued and required for an honorable marriage. *Taupous* were ceremonial virgins and were accorded high rank; they were erotically adorned and considered marriageable prizes. The *taupou* system continued as a custom during Mead's time, but she explained it in light of her own beliefs about the liberal Samoan attitude toward sex. She said it was part of the convention of "promiscuity before marriage" because it took the "onus of virginity" off "the whole young female population" and placed it on the *taupou*.

In fact, retaining one's virginity before marriage was de rigueur for all the adolescent girls in that sternly Christian setting. There had been public defloration ceremonies in pagan Samoa, and though such ceremonies no longer occurred in Mead's time, the "cult of virginity" had a lasting impact on Samoan values. For example, a nubile adolescent girl was commonly guarded by her brothers, particularly at night, against men who might seek to deprive her of her virginity; this hardly jibed with the libertine world described by Mead.

When E. B. Tylor's landmark *Primitive Culture* came out in 1871, the discipline of anthropology was primarily influenced by evolutionism, the belief that the processes of biological evolution were responsible for the course of human cultural history. That the complexity of cultural experience could be so naively ascribed to the laws of biology and "nature" inflamed academics like Boas, who later built his career on denying and challenging this notion.

A major shift in evolutionism occurred in 1889, when August Weissman, from the University of Freiburg, and other experimental biologists brought about the demise of the theory of inheritance of acquired characteristics. Until then, this type of inheritance had been regarded, even to some degree by Darwin, as the primary mode of social evolution, and it was characterized by swift change.

This shift led to the formation of two distinct schools of thought about the development of human societies. "Social Darwinists" saw natural selection as the process that determined the nature of all life on earth and in the cosmos. Benjamin Kidd, a prominent Social Darwinist of the 1890s, summarized this standpoint when he wrote, "Not only is the cosmic process everywhere triumphant but our ethical and moral progress have no meaning apart from it; they are mere phases of it, developed, as every phase of life from the beginning has been, on the strictest and sternest conditions of Natural Selection." The opposing view held that the dynamic of culture was separate from biological processes and that human social history was not governed by natural selection.

However, the distinction between what is biological and what is cultural ought not to be given up, for it is necessary if we wish to understand causes and mechanisms of change. In his Margaret Mead and Samoa study, for instance, Freeman uses the example of Samoan respect language. This language is comprised of many respectful terms coined for use in the assemblies of chiefs where conflicts would be resolved and where tensions often ran high. Use of these polite terms and expressions ("referring to the bodily parts, possessions, attributes, and actions of both titular and talking chiefs and the members of their families") at times of mounting emotional turmoil could potentially stem outbursts of rage or even violence.

Freeman noted that as use of this specialized language in gatherings of chiefs increased, physiological changes suggesting irritation and smoldering anger became more and more evident. When the formal language could no longer contain the situation, the individuals involved resorted to uncontrolled and aggressive "animal-like" behavior. Hence, the origin of Samoan respect language can be understood as a coping response to the tensions created by the Samoan social structure (characterized by rank and dominance). The anger response provoked by these tensions, however, is genetically programmed and inherited.

The ultimate recognition of the significance of *both* biology and culture in human nature can be represented by an interesting metaphor, for half of which Mead and Ruth Benedict (a disciple and former student of Boas and a mentor to Mead) were responsible. In Benedict's zeal to portray culture as "personality writ large," she borrowed the term *Apollonian* from Nietzsche's *The Birth of Tragedy* to describe those who escape "disruptive psychological states" and achieve the ideals of equanimity and moderation. Mead, with Benedict's blessing, chose to describe the Samoans with this term, lauding their society's "elaborate, impersonal structure" and its harmonious consequences for their people. However, both Mead and Benedict selectively ignored or failed to grasp that Nietzsche had posited a partnership between the Apollonian and the Dionysian. The latter, referring to the earthly, primitive, and irreducible aspect of human nature, coexists with order, balance, and the higher sensibilities, just as the gods Dionysus and Apollo resided together at the temple in Delphi. It seems logical to assume that neither Nietzsche nor even the ancient Greeks would have thought much of Boas's paradigm.

Chapter 4: Early Differences

Low birth weight (LBW) is more common in less affluent regions. Many of the characteristics of LBW children are the same as those of children brought up in relatively deprived conditions—they are more likely to have suboptimal diets, a higher risk of infection, inadequate medical care, a lack of intellectual stimulation, poor education, and low drive. The best predictor of LBW is that the mother is living in poverty. In Great Britain, 4.8 percent of all babies born to "class 1" (what we'd call upper-class) mothers are LBW babies, while 15.2 percent of the babies born to "class 4" (lower-class) mothers are low birth weight.

Preterm babies who are the appropriate weight for their gestation age catch up, while the small-for-date (SFD) babies are unlikely to. There is no clear difference between the prognosis for the mental development of premature versus SFD babies; both tend to have reading and learning difficulties. Similarly, both are more likely to have behavioral problems. There are more battered babies among LBWs.

We can divide low-birth-weight babies into three types: (1) those caused by mothers with toxemia, renal disease, advanced hypertension, or diabetes—these babies have a generally good prognosis; (2) those born too soon who have a different problem but follow a similar pattern (some of these may have been induced early for medical reasons); (3) those with chromosome abnormalities, tetragens (substances toxic to pregnant mothers), or intrauterine infections, especially rubella, for whom there is a poor prognosis.

One study of preterm babies found that mothers had problems with early bonding to their children who were initially kept in a special-care baby unit with tubes, wires, bright lights, and all the rest. Moreover, having a premature baby was often a crisis for the mother, for whom memories of earlier miscarriages or infant deaths could be reawakened. So there was likely to be a separation from the baby, psychologically if not physically. Many mothers reported feeling that such a small child was "not me," not human, more like a skinned rabbit, and they didn't want to touch the baby. Such anxieties persisted until school age for many mothers. LBW babies born to middle-class mothers and who had a good relationship with a caregiver did fairly well.

Later in life, the intelligence of LBW babies suffers. Twins have lower birth weight than singles, and twins, on the average, test nine points lower on IQ than singletons and weigh an average of 320 grams less at birth. LBW babies also have a lower resistance to infection and higher rate of death. One-third of the survivors have significant motor and mental handicaps. They have more likelihood of abnormalities. The lower the birth weight, the smaller the child is likely to be later.

Chapter 5: Three Dimensions of Temperament

I've integrated a great deal of work here, but my presentation isn't radically different from what has been determined through factor analysis of testing results. A summary of work from the thousands, if not hundreds of thousands or even millions, of people who have taken the **MMPI** (Minnesota Multiphase Personality Inventory) as well as other tests supports the idea, with which most psychologists agree, that there are five main areas that define personality: extroversion/introversion is one factor; neuroticism is another; openness to experience is a third; sociability is a fourth; and conscientiousness is a fifth.

People also differ in their tendency to perceive their own behavior as internally or externally controlled. Julian Rotter made possible systematic investigation into this perceived *locus of control* by devising the Internal-External (I-E) scale. This questionnaire examines a person's sense of control over personal achievement and over social and political events. The subject must choose between two items such as:

> Becoming a success is a matter of hard work; luck has little or nothing to do with it.
> *or*
> Getting a good job depends mainly on being in the right place at the right time.

> No matter how hard you try, some people just don't like you.
> *or*
> People who can't get others to like them don't understand how to get along with others.

People who perceive events as situationally caused or due to luck are *externals. Internals* believe that events are under personal control. An *internal* would most likely pick "Becoming a success is a matter of hard work . . . " and "People who can't get others to like them. . . ."

There are some very interesting differences between externals and internals. Externals are less likely to delay gratification, they are more susceptible to manipulation, and they are less likely to notice their environment (Lefcourt, 1976). Demographically, men are more internal than women. Internality increases with age, and minorities and lower socioeconomic groups are more external than higher socioeconomic groups.

Consider two people at the extremes. An older, white, wealthy male most likely believes that he has personal control over events. A young, poor, black woman is less likely to perceive that she has personal control over life. She is likely to believe that what happens to her is a matter of luck or external forces. And, unfortunately, they are both likely to be correct!

Chapter 8: Positive Approach, Negative Withdrawal

Some people seem just to burst out in emotions throughout their lives. Is this just our perception of them, or is emotional explosiveness something stable? Bar-Lev Caspi reviewed a fifty-year study of people with data gathered in Berkeley. He found that people who are explosive in early childhood stay that way. This trait shapes their lives to some extent: they are quickly fired, they are twice as likely to become divorced, and they get less education. Whether temper is inherited is still unclear, but it might well relate to activity level in infancy. While this may well be a small dimension of personality, it shows that people can be consistent in certain behaviors.

Chapter 9: Disorders

In the 1940s the psychiatrist William Sheldon advanced his own "body-type" theory of personality in which he classified three basic types of human individuals: ectomorphs are lean, delicate people who are quiet and nonassertive; endomorphs are buxom and peaceful; and mesomorphs are muscular and combative. Further, Sheldon measured the proportions of hundreds of boys he categorized as juvenile delinquents and concluded that they were generally mesomorphs. Sheldon's critics challenged his data.

Another biological theory of crime is that males with an extra Y chromosome (XYY) are more prone to commit criminal acts than XY males. However, there is no convincing evidence to support this, and at least one geneticist has proposed that the condition is more common than we might guess: perhaps one in every 250 males has an extra Y chromosome. XYY status has been brought up as a defense in a few murder trials, but it has not succeeded.

At the end of the last century, the psychological basis of crime became an area of study. Theories fell into one of two categories: crime as a means of holding off mental illness and crime as the result of mental illness. In the first case, people were thought to turn to crime to express their frustration, assert their ability to control their destiny, and thus keep their sanity from slipping away.

Freud implicated guilt as "the real motor of crime" after a number of his upstanding patients confessed they had committed crimes, some as children, some as adults. Through psychoanalysis, Freud deduced that they had transgressed out of a desire to do what was forbidden and that the unidentifiable guilt each one had possessed prior to the crime was assuaged after the crime had been committed.

Other psychoanalysts point to the need for self-affirmation as a trigger. Karl Menninger recounted the story of a nineteen-year-old Australian boy who, following his attempt to assassinate a politician, said to the police, "I realized that unless I did something out of the ordinary I would remain a nobody all my life." Similarly, the ancient Greek Herostratus justified the act of torching the temple of Artemis at Ephesus by stating that he needed to carve his name into history so that he would be forever remembered.

That schizophrenia is more widespread in and around cities rather than in rural regions has always been attributed to the urban drift of early-stage schizophrenics. However, a study by Swedish researchers has shown that the city environment itself is a risk factor for the illness. This means that schizophrenia may be both a biological and a social affliction.

This research was based on two data bases. One was a record of psychiatric hospitalizations between 1970 and 1983; using this information, the researchers tallied those who were first-time schizophrenic patients. Then, a data base of eighteen- and nineteen-year-old Swedish males compiled from 1969 to 1970 provided information on where these hospitalized individuals had been raised. Those who had an urban background represented a significantly larger proportion of the schizophrenic patients than those who came from the woods. Family history of mental illness, economic stress, and parent divorce were controlled variables.

Nearsightedness appears to be linked to **IQ**. Early reports of myopia among intellectual groups can be found from as early as 1813, when it was observed that the British navy had more nearsighted officers than men of lower rank. In Iceland, almost one-half of honors graduates from colleges wear glasses. At the University of California, Berkeley, half the students are nearsighted, while myopes represent only 10 percent of the general population.

Myopes have an intelligence of about one standard deviation higher than the rest of the population, and their **IQ** range is much, much higher. Interestingly, students who become myopic at ages seventeen to eighteen have already achieved their full **IQ** advantage by age eight. What this means is that the intelligence gain must be caused by something that also causes myopia, rather than myopia causing the intelligence gain. There is no question that myopia is dependent on hereditary factors because there is complete concordance between myopia and identical twins while there is much less correlation in twins who don't share genes to the same extent. Thus, myopia follows the classic inheritance pattern.

Chapter 12: Sex Matters

Finding males at their "peak fertility" is not relevant to females seeking mates because males maintain their reproductive ability at a fairly steady level throughout postpubertal life. Thus, the prediction is that men would want as mates women exhibiting the physical features indicative of their peak fertility years—that is, the features of youth, such as "smooth skin, good muscle tone, lustrous hair, and full lips"— and they would look for behavioral characteristics such as "high energy level and sprightly gait." These are all the standard features associated with physical attractiveness.

There are two possibilities for the ages of women whom males might seek: men might prefer women just reaching puberty, who have all of their reproductive lives—and therefore, children—ahead of them. Or they might prefer to mate with women at peak fertility, who are likely to produce offspring very soon. In either case, the "best-choice" female would be close to maximal reproduction age.

David Buss proposes that genetically motivated mate preferences manifest in our society as males competing to display their resources to women and women competing to display their reproductive ability to men. Although there is no scientific proof as yet of such behavior, you can judge from your own observations of humans whether the idea has merit: males, for example, engage in more competition for social status than females do, represented in their higher mortality rates from engaging in showy risk-taking behavior, such as fighting and automobile racing.

One reason males need to dominate lies not only in their vulnerability (more die at any age than women and they live less long) but also in the fact that they can't completely be sure who is the father of a child. Identification of one's genetic offspring is essential to investing appropriately in them. Females always know who their offspring are, except in the odd case of switches in the hospital.

But males cannot be completely confident that a specific woman is bearing their offspring unless they control sexual access to a particular female. Consequently, in order to secure rights to children, men must first secure rights to women. Physical domination and the control of other valuable resources is one way to gain access to children.

If it is true, as some propose, that men are more likely to commit rape because it fits with their genetically born desire to engage in frequent reproductive behavior, then that still does not, by any stretch of the imagination, make rape condonable. It is fully within the capacity of human beings to exert conscious control over any urge, regardless of whether its source lies in evolved biological tendencies, immediate drives like hunger or thirst, or psychologically based desires.

Bibliography

Adler, A. (1929). *The Practice and Theory of Individual Psychology.* New York: Harcourt.

Albert, M. A., and Obler, L. K. (1978). *The Bilingual Brain.* New York: Academic Press.

Allen, L. S., and Gorski, R. A. (1992). "Sexual Orientation and the Size of the Anterior Commissure in the Human Brain." *Proceedings of the National Academy of Science,* 89 (15): 7199–202.

American Psychiatric Association. (1980). *Diagnostic and Statistical Manual of Mental Disorders.* (3rd ed.) Washington, DC: American Psychiatric Association.

Annett, M., and Annett, J. (1991)."Handedness for Eating in Gorillas." *Cortex* 27 (2): 269–75.

Annett, M. (1991). "Laterality and Cerebral Dominance." *Journal of Child Psychology and Psychiatry* 32 (2): 219–32.

Annett, M., and Manning, M. (1990). "Arithmetic and Laterality." *Neuropsychologia* 28 (1): 61–9.

Annett, M., and Manning, M. (1989). "The Disadvantages of Dextrality for Intelligence." *British Journal of Psychology* 80 (Part 2): 213–26 Unique.

Annett, M. (1991.) "Speech Lateralization and Phonological Skill." *Cortex* 27 (4): 583–93.

Baddeley, A. (1986). *Working Memory.* New York: Oxford University Press.

Bahrick, H. P., Bahrick, P. O., and Whittlinger, R. P. (1975). "Fifty Years of Memory for Names and Faces: A Cross-sectional Approach." *Journal of Experimental Psychology: General* 104, 54–75.

Barsley, M. (1979). *Left-handed People.* North Hollywood, CA: Wilshire.

Baumeister, R. F. (1987). "How the Self Became a Problem: A Psychological Review of Historical Research." *Journal of Personality and Social Psychology* 52, 163–76.

Baxter, L. R., and others. (1992). "Caudate Glucose Metabolic Rate Changes with Both Drug and Behavior Therapy for Obsessive-Compulsive Disorder." *Archives of General Psychiatry* 49, 681–89.

Beatty, W. W. (1979). "Gonadal Hormones and Sex Differences in Nonreproductive Behavior in Rodents: Organizational and Activational Influences." *Hormones and Behavior* 12, 112–63.

Belsky, J., Steinberg, L., and Draper, P. (1991). "Childhood Experience, Interpersonal Development, and Reproductive Strategy: An

Evolutionary Theory of Socialization." *Child Development* 62 (4): 647–70.

Belsky, J. (1984). "The Determinants of Parenting: A Process Model." *Child Development* 55, 83–96.

Bjork, R. A., and Landauer, T. K. (1979). "On Keeping Track of the Present Status of People and Things." In M. M. Gruneberg, P. E. Morris, and R. N. Sykes (eds.), *Practical Aspects of Memory.* New York: Academic Press.

Bouchard, T., and McGue, R. (1981). "Familial Studies of Intelligence: A Review." *Science* 212, 1055–59.

Breuer, J., and Freud, S. (1955). "Studies in Hysteria." In J. Strachey (ed.), *The Standard Edition of the Complete Psychological Works of Sigmund Freud.* London: Hogarth Press. (Original work published 1895.)

Brown, J. R., and Dunn, J. (1992). "Talk with Your Mother or Your Sibling? Developmental Changes in Early Family Conversations About Feelings." *Child Development* 63 (2): 336–49.

Brown, D. M. (1990). *Human Universals.* New York: McGraw-Hill.

Burges, I. P., Hoffman, L., and Wilson, G. V. (1988). "The Neuropsychiatry of Posttraumatic Stress Disorder." *British Journal of Psychiatry* 152, 164–73.

Buss, A. H., Plomin, R., and Willerman, L. (1973). "The Inheritance of Temperaments." *Journal of Personality* 41, 513–24.

Buss, A. H., and Plomin, R. (1984). *Temperament: Early-Developing Personality Traits.* Hillsdale, NJ: Erlbaum.

Buss, D. (1989). "Sex Differences in Human Mate Preferences." *Brain and Behavioral Sciences* 12 (1): 1–38.

Carughi, A., Carpenter, K. J., and Diamond, M. C. (1989) "Effect of Environmental Enrichment During Nutritional Rehabilitation on Body Growth, Blood Parameters, and Cerebral Cortical Development of Rats." *Journal of Nutrition* 119, 2005–16.

Carver, C. S., and Scheier, M. F. (1988). *Perspectives on Personality.* Boston: Allyn & Bacon.

Cattell, R. B. (1971). *Abilities: Their Structure, Growth, and Action.* Boston: Houghton Mifflin.

Chrousos, G. P., and Gold, P. W. (1992). "The Concepts of Stress and Stress Systems Disorders: Overview of Physical and Behavioral Homeostasis." *JAMA* 267, 1244–52.

Claridge, G. (1985). *Origins of Mental Illness: Temperament, Deviance, and Disorder.* New York: Basil Blackwell.

Connor, J. R., and Diamond, M. C. (1982). "A Comparison of Dendritic Spine Number and Type on Pyramidal Neuron of the Visual Cortex of Old Adult Rats from Social and Isolated Environments." *Journal of Comparative Neurology* 210, 99–106.

Coren, S. (1989). "Left-handedness and Accident-Related Injury Risk." *American Journal of Public Health* 79 (8): 1040–41.

Costa, P. T., and McCrae, R. R. (1980). "Still Stable After All These Years: Personality as a Key to Some Issues in Adulthood and Old Age." In P. Baltes and O. Brim (eds.), *Life-span Development and Behavior.* Vol. 3. New York: Academic Press.

Costa, P., and McCrae, R. (1984). *Emerging Lives, Enduring Dispositions.* New York: Guilford Press.

Craik, F. (1977). "Age Differences in Human Memory." In J. Birren and K. Schaie (eds.), *Handbook of the Psychology of Aging.* New York: Van Nostrand Reinhold.

Damasio, A. (1979). "The Frontal Lobes." In K. M. Heilman and E. Valenstein (eds.), *Clinical Neuropsychology.* New York: Oxford University Press.

Darwin, C. (1968). *On the Origin of Species.* New York: Penguin Books. (Original work published 1859).

Darwin, C. (1872). *The Expression of the Emotions in Man and Animals.* London: Longmans.

Davidson, R. (1984). "Hemispheric Asymmetry and Emotion." In K. Scherer and P. Ekman (eds.), *Approaches to Emotion.* Hillsdale, NJ: Erlbaum.

Davis, M. R., and Fernald, R. D. (1990). "Social Control and Neuronal Soma Size." *Journal of Neurobiology* 21, 1180–8.

DeKay, W. T., and Buss, D. M. (1992). "Human Nature, Individual Differences, and the Importance of Context: Perspectives from Evolutionary Psychology." *Current Directions in Psychological Science* 1 (6): 184–9.

Diamond, M. C. (1980). "Environment, Air Ions, and Brain Chemistry." *Psychology Today* (June): 38–44.

Donald, M. (1991). *Origins of the Modern Mind: Three Stages in the Evolution of Culture and Cognition.* Cambridge, MA: Harvard University Press.

Draper, P., and Belsky, J. (1990). "Personality Development in the Evolutionary Perspective." *Journal of Personality* 58 (1): 141–61.

Dua, P. S. (1970). "Comparison of the Effects of Behaviorally Oriented Action and Psychotherapy Reeducation on Introversion-Extroversion, Emotionality, and Internal-External Control." *Journal of Counseling Psychology* 17, 567–72.

Dunn, J. F., Plomin, R., and Daniels, D. (1986). "Consistency and Change in Mothers' Behavior Toward Young Siblings." *Child Development* 57 (2): 348–56.

Dunn, J., and Kendrick, C. (1982). "Temperamental Differences, Family Relationships, and Young Children's Response to Change Within the Family." *Ciba Foundation Symposium* 89, 87–105.

Dunn, J., and Munn, P. (1986). "Sibling Quarrels and Maternal Intervention: Individual Differences in Understanding and Aggression." *Journal of Child Psychology and Psychiatry* 27 (5): 583–95.

Dunn, J., and Plomin, R. (1990). *Separate Lives: Why Siblings Are So Different*. New York: Basic Books.

Earls, F., and Jung, K. G. (1987). "Temperament and Home Environment Characteristics as Causal Factors in the Early Development of Childhood Psychopathology." *Journal of the American Academy of Child and Adolescent Psychiatry* 26, 491–8.

Ehrlich, P. R., and Feldman, S. S. (1977). *The Race Bomb: Skin Color, Prejudice, and Intelligence*. New York: Quadrangle/New York Times Book Company.

Eysenck, J. J. (1979). "The Conditioning Model of Neurosis." *Behavioral and Brain Sciences* 2, 155–99.

Fausto-Sterling, A. (1986). *Myths of Gender: Biological Theories About Women and Men*. New York: Basic Books.

Fendrich, R., and Gazzaniga, M. S. (1989). "Evidence of Foveal Splitting in a Commissurotomy Patient." *Neuropsychologia* 27 (3): 273–81.

Flor-Henry, P. (1985). "Psychiatric Aspects of Cerebral Lateralization." *Psychiatric Annuals* 15, 429–34.

Fox, N. A., and Davidson, R. (1986). "Taste-elicited Changes in Facial Signs of Emotion and the Asymmetry of Brain Electrical Activity in Human Newborns." *Neuropsychologia* 24 (3): 417–22.

Freeman, D. (1983). *Margaret Mead and Samoa*. Cambridge, MA: Harvard University Press.

Freud, S. (1966). "The Neuropsychoses of Defense." In James Strachey, ed., *Standard Edition of the Complete Psychological Works of Sigmund Freud,* Vol. 1. London: Hogarth Press, 45–65. (Original work published 1894.)

Freud, S. (1966). "Further Remarks on the Neuropsychoses of Defense." In *Standard Edition,* Vol. 3, 159. (Original work published 1896.)

Freud, S. (1966). "Beyond the Pleasure Principle." In *Standard Edition,* Vol. 18. (Original work published 1920.)

Freud, S. (1955). *The Interpretation of Dreams*. London: Hogarth Press. (Original work published 1900.)

Friedman, M. J. (1988). "Toward Rational Pharmacotherapy for Posttraumatic Stress Disorder: An Interim Report." *American Journal of Psychiatry* 145, 281–5.

Fuster, J. M. (1985). "The Frontal Lobes, Mediator of Cross-temporal Contingencies." *Human Neurobiology* 4, 169–79.

Galin, D., Ornstein, R. E., Herron, J., and Johnstone, J. (1982). "Sex and Handedness Differences in EEG Measures of Hemispheric Specialization." *Brain and Language* 16 (1): 19–55.

Galin, D., and Ornstein, R. (1972). "Lateral Specialization of Cognitive Mode: An EEG Study." *Psychophysiology* 9, 412–8.

Gardner, H. (1983). *Frames of Mind*. New York: Basic Books.

Gershon, E. S., and Rieder, R. O. (1992) "Major Disorders of Mind and Brain." *Scientific American* 267, 126–33.

Goleman, D. (1990). "A Key to Posttraumatic Stress Disorder Lies in Brain Chemistry, Scientists Say." *New York Times,* June 12, p. C1.

Goleman, D. (1989). "What Is Negative About Positive Illusions? When Benefits for the Individual Harm the Collective." *Journal of Social and Clinical Psychology* 8, 190–7.

Gottesman, I. I. (1962). "Differential Inheritance of the Psychoneuroses." *Eugenics Quarterly* 9, 223–7.

Gottesman, I. I. (1968). "Severity/Concordance and Diagnostic Refinement in the Mandsely-Bethlem Schizophrenic Twin Study." In D. Rosenthal and S. S. Kety (eds.), *The Transmission of Schizophrenia.* New York: Pergamon Press.

Gottesman, I. I. (1991). *Schizophrenia Genesis: The Origins of Madness.* New York: W. H. Freeman.

Gottesman, I. I., and Shields, J. (1972). *Schizophrenia and Genetics: A Twin Study Vantage Point.* New York: Academic Press.

Gray, J. A. (1984). *The Neuropsychology of Anxiety.* New York: Oxford University Press.

Greeno, C. G., and Maccoby, E. (1986). "How Different Is the 'Different' Voice?" *Signs* 11 (2): 310–16.

Hall, C. S., and Lindzey, G. (1978). *Theories of Personality.* (3rd ed.) New York: Wiley.

Halpern, D. (1992). *Sex Differences in Cognitive Abilities.* Hillsdale, NJ: LEA.

Halpern, D. F., and Coren, S. (1988). "Do Right-handers Live Longer?" (Letter). *Nature* 333 (6170): 213.

Hamilton, W. D. (1964). "The Genetical Evolution of Social Behavior." *Journal of Theoretical Biology* 7, 1–52.

Harpending, H., and Draper, P. (1990). "Estimating Parity of Parents: Application to the History of Infertility Among the !Kung of Southern Africa." *Human Biology* 62 (2): 195–203.

Hartmann, H. (1958). *Ego Psychology and the Problem of Adaptation.* New York: International Universities Press. (Original work published 1939.)

Herrmann, D. J., and Neisser, U. (1978). "An Inventory of Everyday Memory Experiences." In M. M. Gruneberg, P. E. Morris, and R. N. Sykes (eds.), *Practical Aspects of Memory.* New York: Academic Press.

Herrnstein, R. J. (1973). *IQ in the Meritocracy.* Boston: Little, Brown.

Horwitz, B., Swedo, S. E., Grady, C. L., Pietrini, P., and others. (1991). "Cerebral Metabolic Pattern in Obsessive-Compulsive Disorder: Altered Intercorrelations Between Regional Rates of Glucose Utilization." *Psychiatry Research* 40 (4): 221–37.

Insel, T. R., (1992). "Toward a Neuroanatomy of Obsessive-Compulsive Disorder." *Archives of General Psychiatry* 49, 739–44.

Jenkins, W. M., and Merzenich, M. M. (1987). "Reorganization of Neocortical Representations After Brain Injury: A

Neurophysiological Model of the Bases of Recovery from Stroke." *Progress in Brain Research* 71, 249–66.

Jensen, A. R. (1980). *Bias in Mental Testing.* New York: Free Press.

Jensen, A. R. (1969). "How Much Can We Boost IQ and Scholastic Achievement?" *Harvard Educational Review* 39, 1–123.

Joseph, R. (1982). "The Neuropsychology of Development: Hemispheric Laterality, Limbic Language, and the Origin of Thought." *Journal of Clinical Psychology* 38, 4–33.

Kagan, J. (1989). *Unstable Ideas: Temperament, Cognition, and Self.* Cambridge, MA: Harvard University Press.

Kagan, J. (1989). "Temperamental Contributions to Social Behavior." *American Psychologist* 44, 668–83.

Kagan, J., Resnick, J. S., Snidman, N., Gibbons, J., and Johnson, M. C. (1988). "Childhood Derivatives of Inhibition and Lack of Inhibition to the Unfamiliar." *Child Development* 59 (6): 1580–9.

Kagan, J., Resnick, J. S., and Gibbon, J. (1989). "Inhibited and Uninhibited Types of Children." *Child Development* 60 (40): 838–45.

Kagan, J., Snidman, N., and Arcus, D. M. (1992). "Initial Reactions to Unfamiliarity." *Current Directions in Psychological Science* 1 (6): 171–4.

Kandel, E. R., and Hawkins, R. D. (1992). "The Biological Basis of Learning and Individuality." *Scientific American* 267, 78–86.

Kendrick, C., and Dunn, J. (1982). "The Arrival of a Sibling." *Health Visit* 55 (4): 155–7.

Kimura, D. "Sex Differences in Cerebral Organization for Speech and Praxic Functions." *Canadian Journal of Psychology* 37 (1): 19–35.

Kimura, D., and D'Amico, C. "Evidence for Subgroups of Adextrals Based on Speech Lateralization and Cognitive Patterns." *Neuropsychologia* 27 (7): 977–86.

Kimura, D., and Harshman, R. A. (1984). "Sex Differences in Brain Organization for Verbal and Nonverbal Functions." *Progress in Brain Research* 61, 423–41. Unique identifier: BACK83 85141005.

Kosten, T. R., Mason, J. W., Giller, E. L., Ostroff, R. B., and Harkness, L. (1987). "Sustained Urinary Norepinephrine and Epinephrine Elevation in Posttraumatic Stress Disorder." *Psychoneuroendocrinology* 12, 13–20.

Lhermitte, F. (1986). "Human Autonomy and the Frontal Lobes—Part II: Patient Behavior in Complex Social Situations: The 'Environmental Dependency Syndrome.'" *Annals of Neurology* 19, 335–43.

Libet, B. (1985). "Subjective Antedating of a Sensory Experience and Mind-Brain Theories: Reply to Honderich." *Journal of Theoretical Biology* 114 (4): 563–70.

Libet, B. (1989). "The Timing of a Subjective Experience: Reply to Salter." *Behavioral and Brain Sciences* 12 (1): 183–5.

Loehlin, J. C., Willerman, L., and Horn, J. M. (1988). "Human Behavior Genetics." *Annual Review of Psychology* 39, 101–33.

Maccoby, E. (1988). "Gender as a Social Category." *Developmental Psychology* 24, 755–65.

Maccoby, E., and Jacklin, C. N. (1974). *The Psychology of Sex Differences.* Stanford, CA: Stanford University Press.

Malone, T. W. (1983). "How Do People Organize Their Desks? Implications for Designing Office Automation Systems." *ACM Transactions on Office Information Systems* 1, 99–112.

Markus, H. (1983). "Self-knowledge; An Expanded View." *Journal of Personality* 51, 543–65.

Maziade, M., and colleagues. (1990). "Psychiatric Status of Adolescents Who Had Extreme Temperaments at Age Seven." *American Journal of Psychiatry* 147, 1531–6.

McGlone, J. (1980). "Sex Differences in Human Brain Asymmetry: A Critical Survey." *Behavioral and Brain Sciences* 3 (2): 215–63.

Mednick, S. A. (1977). "A Biosocial Theory of the Learning of Law-abiding Behavior." In S. A. Mednick and K. O. Christiansen (eds.), *Biosocial Bases of Criminal Behavior.* New York: Gardner Press.

Merzenich, M. M., and others. (1990). "Adaptive Mechanisms in Cortical Networks Underlying Cortical Contributions to Learning and Nondeclarative Memory." *Cold Spring Harbor Symposia on Quantitative Biology* 55, 873–87.

Merzenich, M. M. (1985). "Sources of Intraspecies and Interspecies Cortical Map Variability in Mammals." In M. Cohen and F. Strumwasser (eds.), *Comparative Neurobiology: Modes of Communication in the Nervous System.* New York: Wiley, 138–57.

North, C. (1987). *Welcome, Silence.* New York: Simon & Schuster.

Ornstein, R. (1986). *Multimind.* Boston: Houghton Mifflin.

Ornstein, R. (1986). *The Psychology of Consciousness.* (3rd ed.) New York: Penguin.

Ornstein, R. (1991). *The Evolution of Consciousness.* New York: Prentice-Hall.

Pilgrim, C., and Reisert, I. (1992). "Differences Between Male and Female Brains: Developmental Mechanisms and Implications." Abteilung Anatomie und Zellbiologie, Universität Ulm, Germany. *Metab Res* 24 (8): 353–8.

Pitman, R. K., van der Kolk, B. A., Orr, S. P., and Greenber, M. S. (1990). "Naloxone-reversible Analgesic Response to Combat-Related Stimuli in Posttraumatic Stress Disorder: A Pilot Study." *Archives of General Psychiatry* 47, 541–4.

Plomin, R. (1989). "Environment and Genes: Determinants of Behavior." *American Psychologist* 44 (2): 105–11.

Plomin, R., and Loehlin, J. C. (1989). "Direct and Indirect IQ Heritability Estimates: A Puzzle." *Behavior Genetics* 19 (3): 331–42.

Plomin, R., and Rowe, D. C. (1977). "A Twin Study of Temperament in Young Children." *Journal of Psychology* 97, 107–13.

Rutter, M., and Caesar, P. (eds.). (1991). *Biological Risk Factors for Psychosocial Disorders.* Cambridge, UK: Cambridge University Press.

Schaffer, C. E., Davidson, R. J., and Saron, C. (1983). "Frontal and Parietal Electroencephalogram Asymmetry in Depressed and Nondepressed Subjects." *Biological Psychiatry* 18, 753–62.

Scheier, M. F., and Carver, C. S. (1987). "Dispositional Optimism and Physical Well-being: The Influence of Generalized Outcome Expectancies on Health." *Journal of Personality* 55 (2): 169–210.

Seligman, M. E. P. (1975). *Helplessness: On Depression, Development, and Death*. San Francisco: W. H. Freeman.

Shapiro, D. (1965). *Neurotic Styles*. New York: Basic Books.

Shatz, C. J. (1992). "The Developing Brain." *Scientific American* 267, 60–7.

Sheehy, M. P., and Marsden, C. D. (1982). "Writer's Cramp: A Focal Dystonia." *Brain* 105, 461–80.

Sternberg, R. J. (1989). *The Triarchic Mind: A New Theory of Human Intelligence*. New York: Penguin.

Stillwell, R., and Dunn, J. (1985). "Continuities in Sibling Relationships: Patterns of Aggression and Friendliness." *Journal of Child Psychology and Psychiatry* 26 (4): 627–37.

Swedo, S. E., and others. (1992). "Cerebral Glucose Metabolism in Childhood-Onset Obsessive-Compulsive Disorder: Revisualization During Pharmacotherapy." *Archives of General Psychiatry* 49, 690–4.

Symons, D. (1980). "Precis of the Evolution of Human Sexuality." *Behavioral and Brain Sciences* 3, 171–214.

Tubman, J. G., Lerner, R. M., Lerner, J. V., and von Eye, A. (1992). "Temperament and Adjustment in Young Adulthood: A Fifteen-Year Longitudinal Analysis." *American Journal of Orthopsychiatry* 62, 564–74.

Tucker, D. M. (1981). "Lateral Brain Function, Emotion, and Conceptualization." *Psychological Bulletin* 89, 19–43.

Van der Kolk, B., Greenber, M., Boyd, H., and Krystal, J. (1985). "Inescapable Shock, Neurotransmitters, and Addiction to Trauma: Toward a Psychobiology of Posttraumatic Stress." *Biological Psychiatry* 20, 314–25.

Walsh, R. N. (1981). "Effects of Environmental Complexity and Deprivation on Brain Anatomy and Histology: A Review." *International Journal of Neuroscience* 12, 33–51.

Watson, N. V., and Kimura, D. (1989). "Right-hand Superiority for Throwing But Not for Intercepting." *Neuropsychologia* 27 (11–12): 1399–414.

Willerman, L. (1979). *The Psychology of Individual and Group Differences*. San Francisco: W. H. Freeman.

Wilson, J. Q., and Herrnstein, R. J. (1985). *Crime and Human Nature*. New York: Simon & Schuster.

Yehuda, R., Giller, E. L., Southwick, S. M., Lowy, M. T., and Mason, J. W. (1991). "Hypothalamic-Pituitary-Adrenal Dysfunction in Posttraumatic Stress Disorder." *Biological Psychiatry* 30, 1031–48.

Zajonc, R. B. (1986). "The Decline and Rise of Scholastic Aptitude Scores."
    American Psychologist 41 (8): 862–7.
Zajonc, R. B., Markus, H., and Markus, G. P. (1979). "The Birth-Order
    Puzzle." *Journal of Personality and Social Psychology* 37, 1325–41.
Zuckerman, M. (1984). "Sensation-seeking: A Comparative Approach to a
    Human Trait." *Brain and Behavioral Sciences* 73, 413–33.

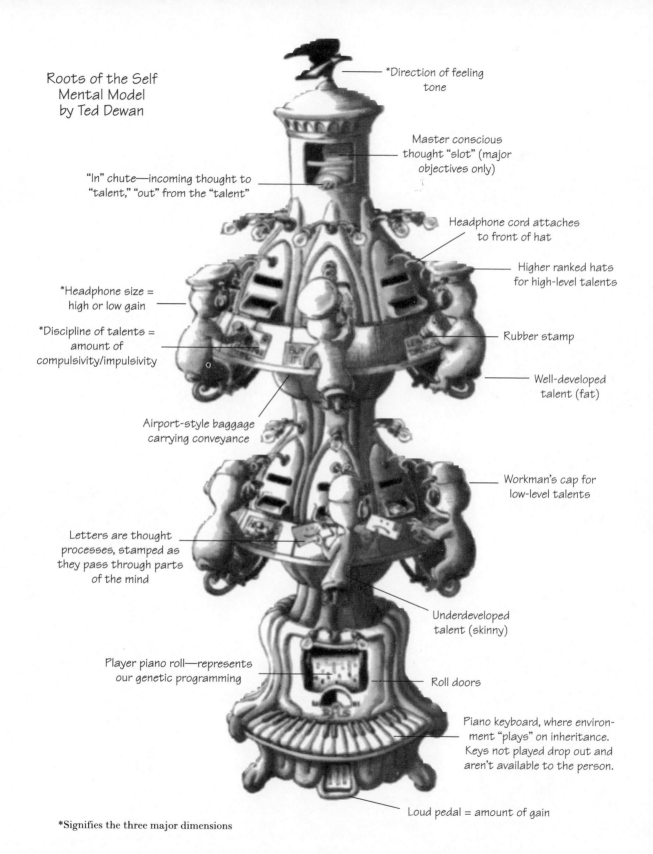

Roots of the Self
Mental Model
by Ted Dewan

*Direction of feeling tone

Master conscious thought "slot" (major objectives only)

"In" chute—incoming thought to "talent," "out" from the "talent"

Headphone cord attaches to front of hat

Higher ranked hats for high-level talents

*Headphone size = high or low gain

*Discipline of talents = amount of compulsivity/impulsivity

Rubber stamp

Well-developed talent (fat)

Airport-style baggage carrying conveyance

Workman's cap for low-level talents

Letters are thought processes, stamped as they pass through parts of the mind

Underdeveloped talent (skinny)

Player piano roll—represents our genetic programming

Roll doors

Piano keyboard, where environment "plays" on inheritance. Keys not played drop out and aren't available to the person.

Loud pedal = amount of gain

*Signifies the three major dimensions

Index

Adler, Alfred, 118

Adolescence, Mead on Samoan, 20-23, 210–11

Adrenaline. *See* Norepinephrine

Affect, 74n

Amplification: continuum of, 52, 53–54; and inhibition, 40. *See also* Gain dimension

Andersen, Hans Christian, 97

Annett, Marian, left-handedness studies of, 157–60

Antisocial personality, as approach-withdrawal extreme, 87–88

Anxiety disorders, as gain extreme, 82–83

Approach-avoidance dimension. *See* Approach-withdrawal dimension

Approach-withdrawal dimension, 5, 73–74, 77; disorders of, 83–88; and hemisphere activity, 74–76; of infants, 39–41

Ascorbic acid, and IQ, 112

Augmentation, 55

Autonomic nervous system (ANS), and criminality, 87

Babies. *See* Infants

Bacon, Francis, 71

Bakan, Paul, 162

Baxter, Lewis, 90–91

Beauvoir, Simone de, 115, 119

Benedict, Ruth, 213

Bigirimana, Antoine, 109

Birth order, 115; and individuality, 118–21

Birth weight. *See* Low birth weight (LBW)

Bleuler, Manfred, 69

Boas, Franz, 19, 209, 211; and Margaret Mead, 20–21, 23

Body type, and personality, 47–48, 216

Bouchard, Thomas, 107

Boundaries: Hartmann's concept of, 67–71; of schizophrenics, 97

Boundaries in the Mind (Hartmann), 67–69

Boy Who Couldn't Stop Washing, The (Rappaport), 90

Brain: and basics of individuality, 48–49; birth size of, 10; as blank slate, 20; change in, 8–9; cultivation of, 182–87; response of, to activities, 7; shaping of, 187–88

Brain damage: in frontal cortex, and OCD, 91–92; in frontal lobes, 66–67; and language, 11; and left-handedness, 161–65

Brain development: and experience, 10–12, 180–82, 183–87; sex differences in, 142

Brain stem, 5, 51–52

Brown, Don, 31, 196

Brown, P. E., 189

Bryden, Marcia, 142

Buss, David, 134, 136, 138, 219

Caspi, Bar-Lev, 216

Catatonia, as gain extreme, 82–83